UNIFORMITY

by the same author
A HUNDRED AND ONE USES OF A DEAD CAT
UNSPEAKABLE ACTS
A HUNDRED AND ONE MORE USES OF A DEAD CAT
ODD VISIONS AND BIZARRE SIGHTS
SUCCESS AND HOW TO BE ONE
TEDDY

SIMON BOND

UNIFORMITY

METHUEN

First published in Great Britain in 1986
by Methuen London Ltd
11 New Fetter Lane, London EC4P 4EE

Copyright © Polycarp Ltd 1986

Made and printed in Great Britain

British Library Cataloguing in Publication Data
Bond, Simon
    Uniformity.
    I. English wit and humor, Pictorial
    I. Title
    741.5'942   NC1479
    ISBN 0-413-41180-X
    ISBN 0-413-41190-7 Pbk

A version of the cartoon on page 23 first appeared in the *New Yorker* in 1986.

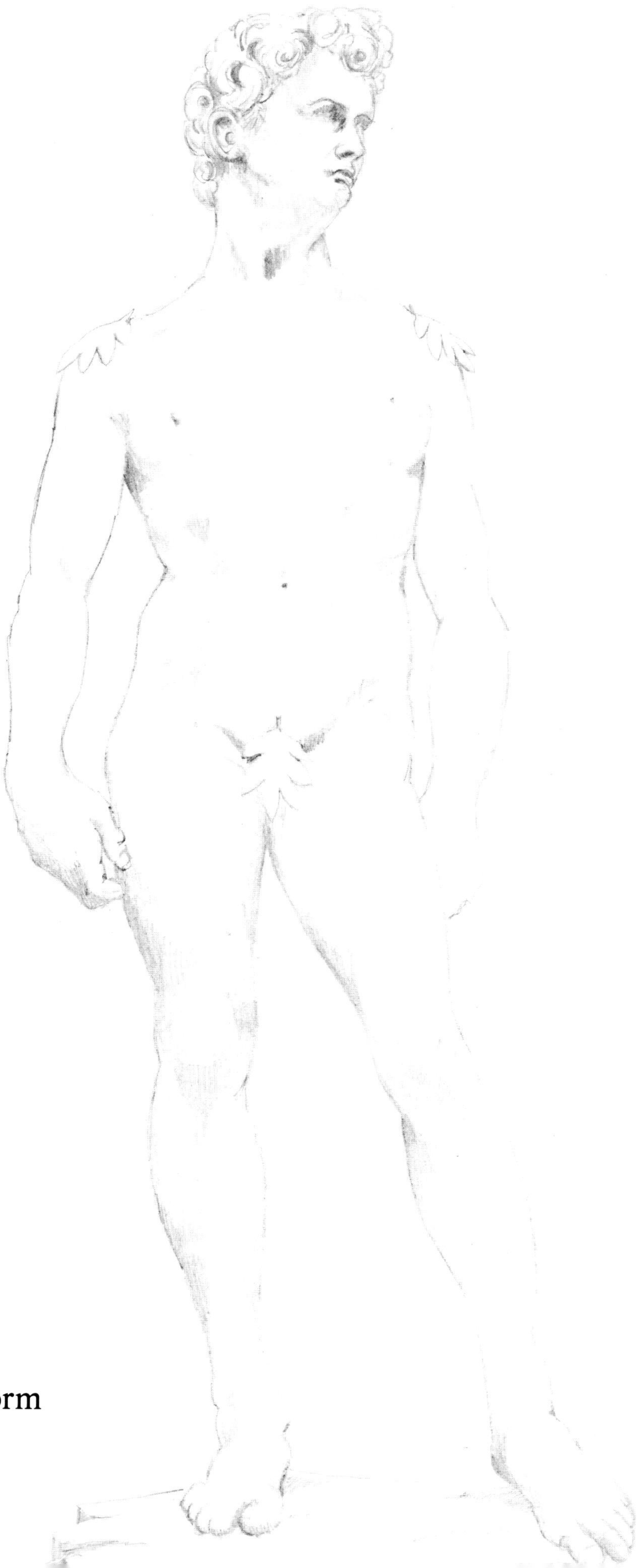

The First Uniform

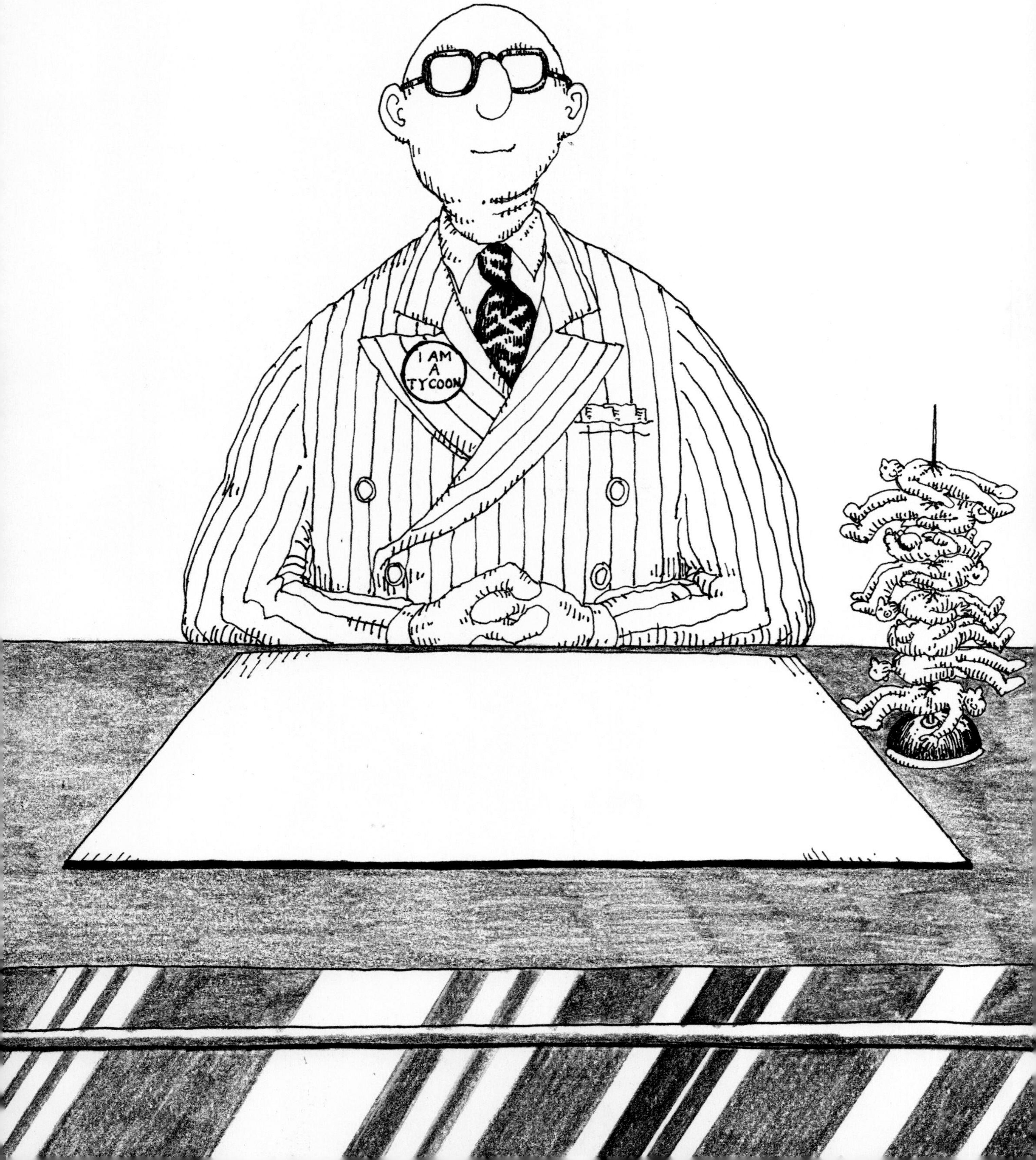
I AM A TYCOON

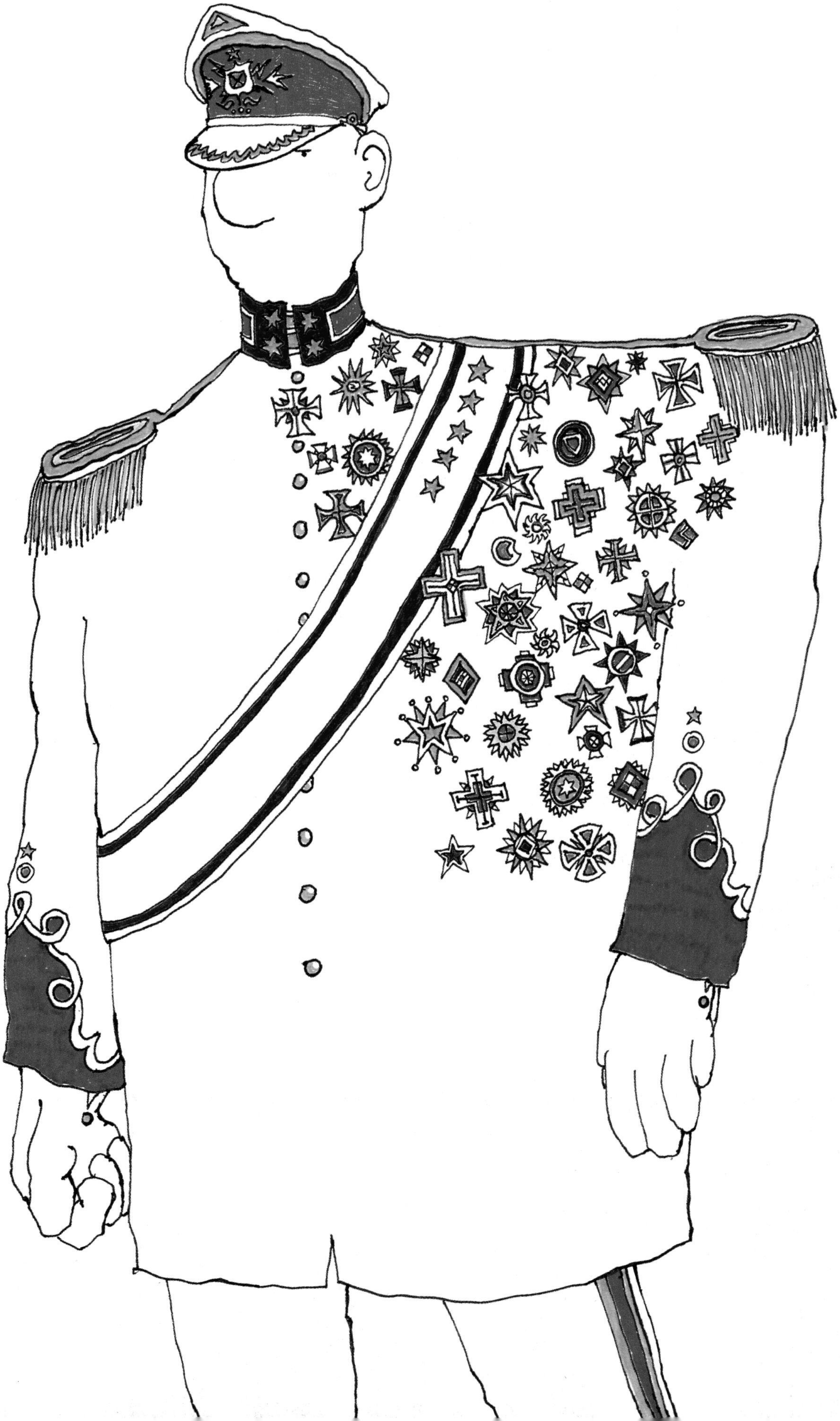

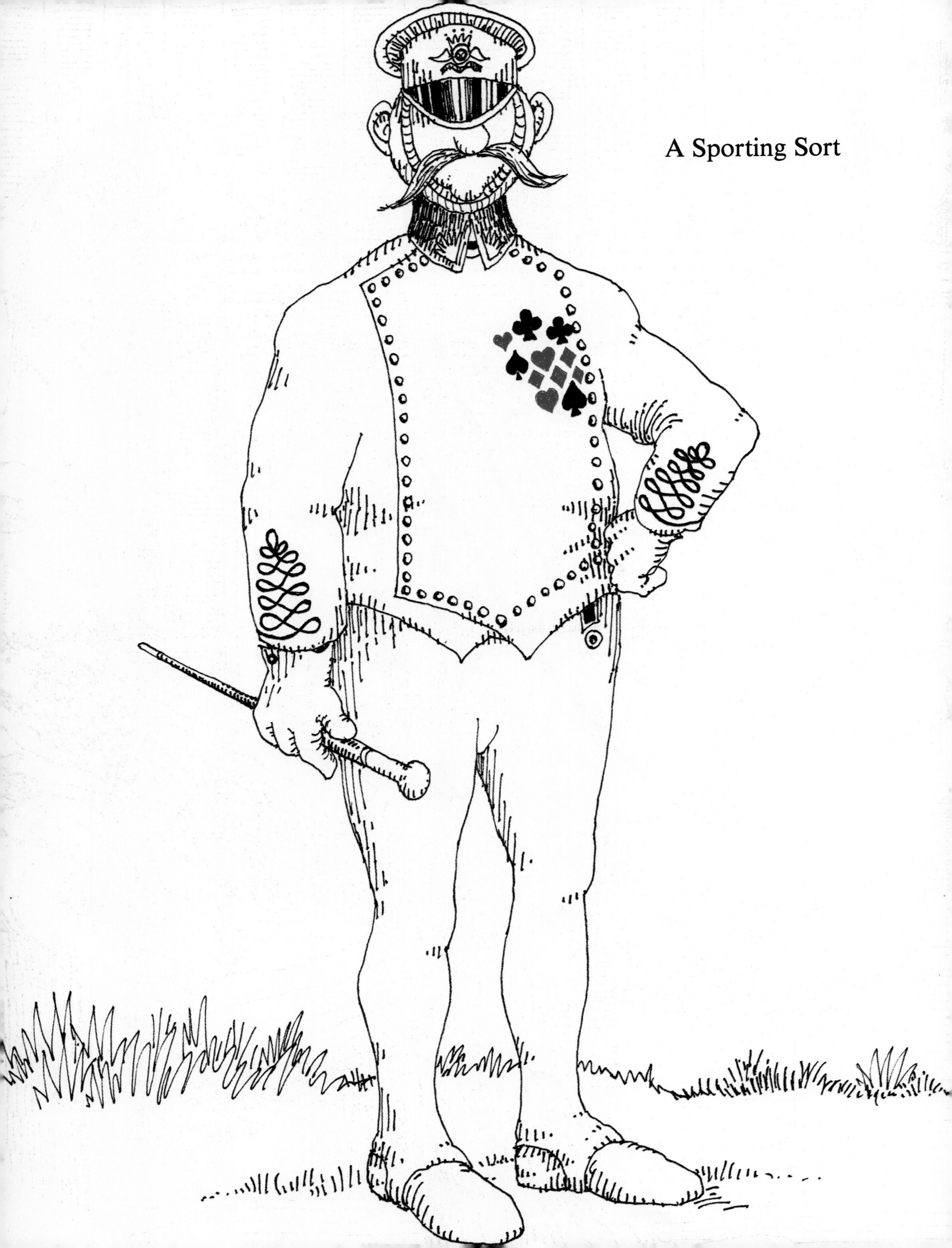

A Sporting Sort

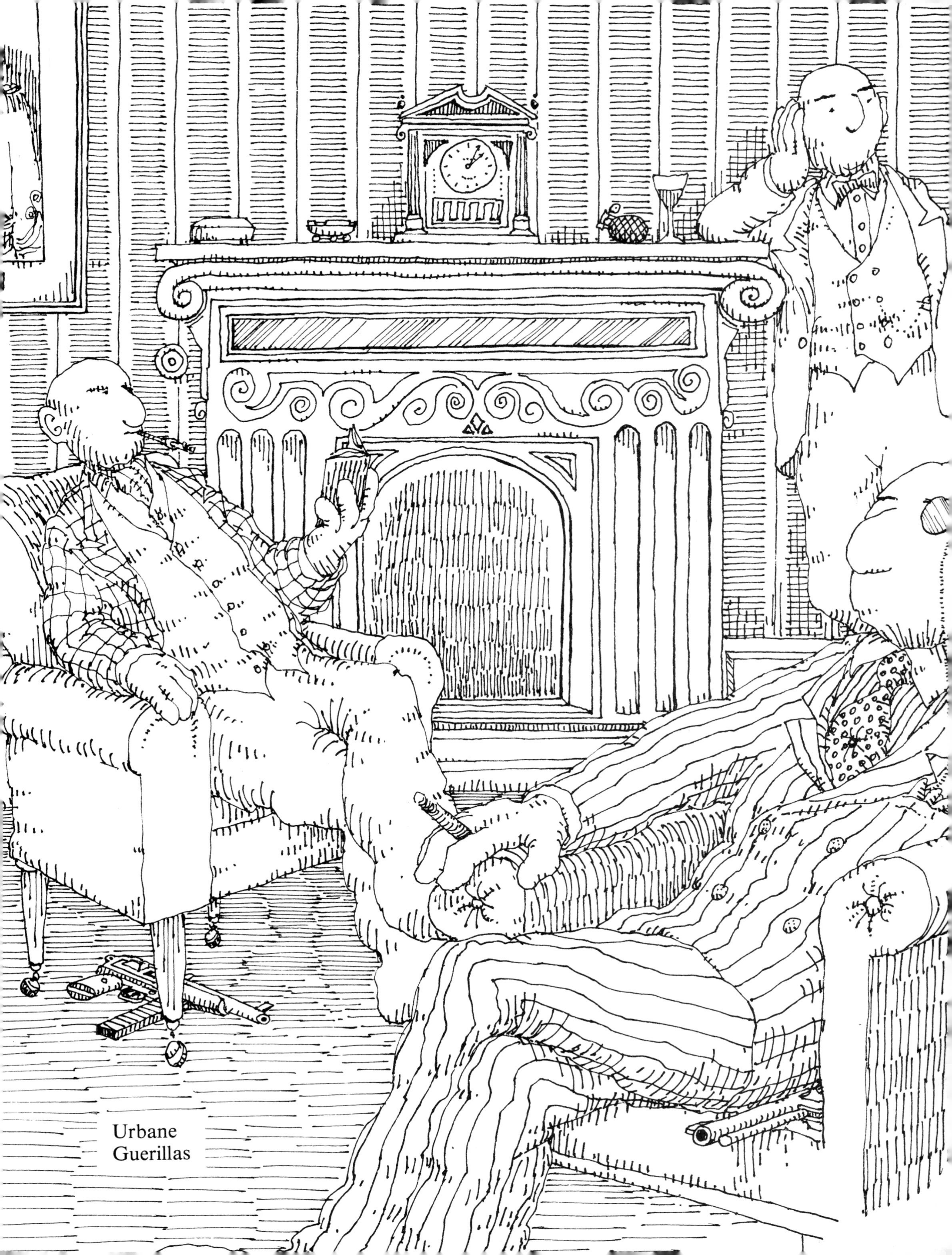

Urbane
Guerillas

Professional Fund Raisers

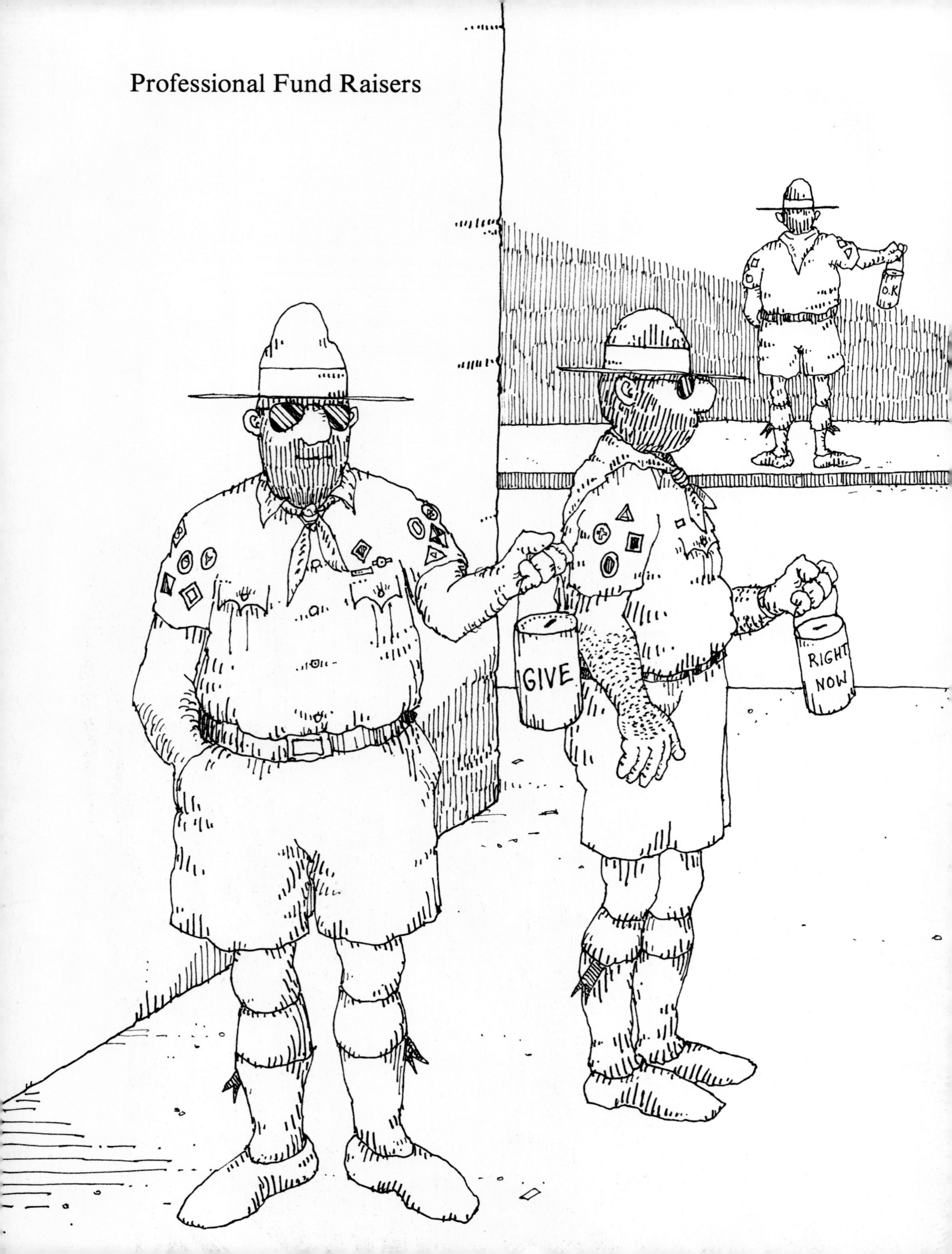
O.K
GIVE
RIGHT NOW

Lord Avariss
Captain of Industry

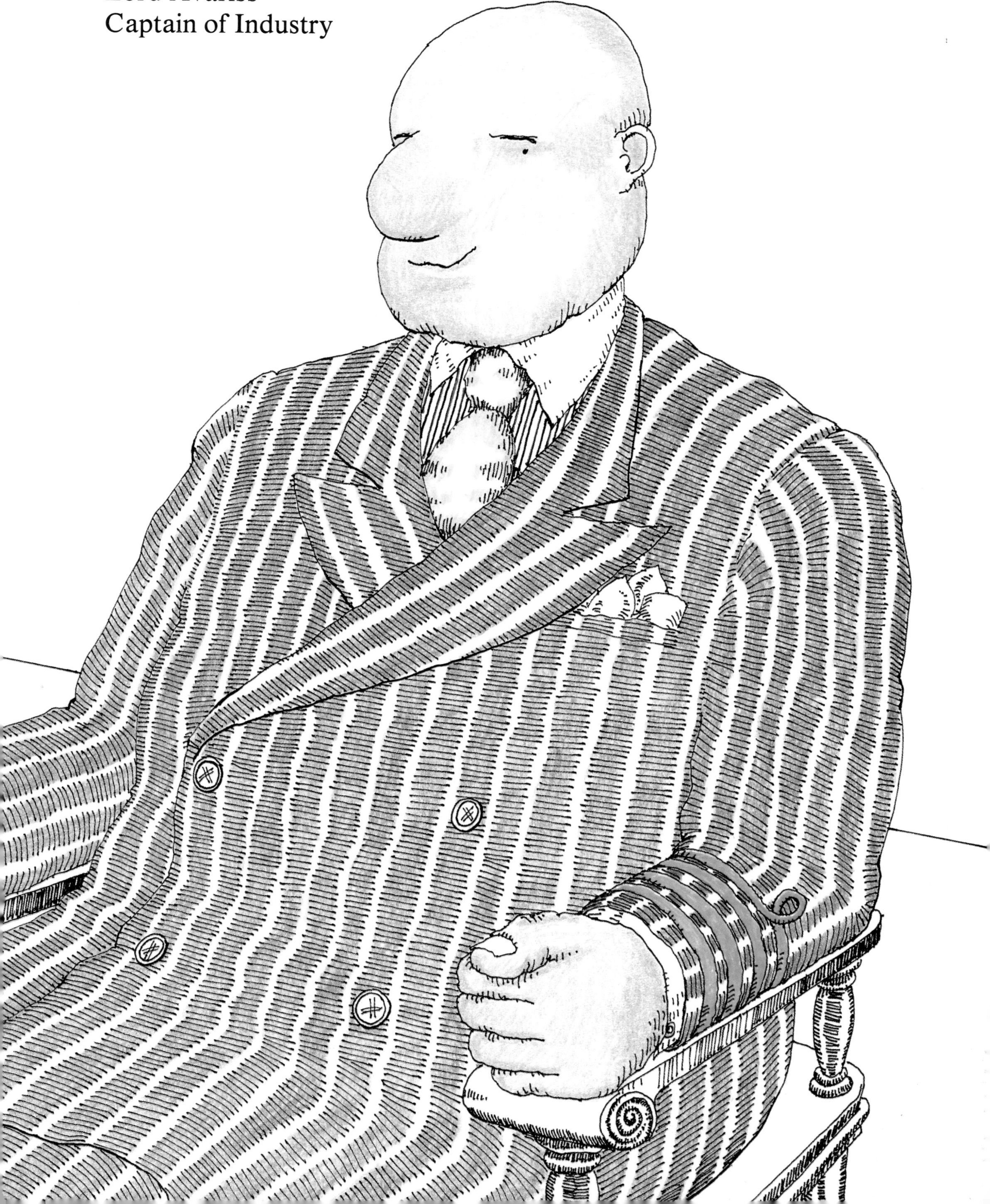

Jealousy

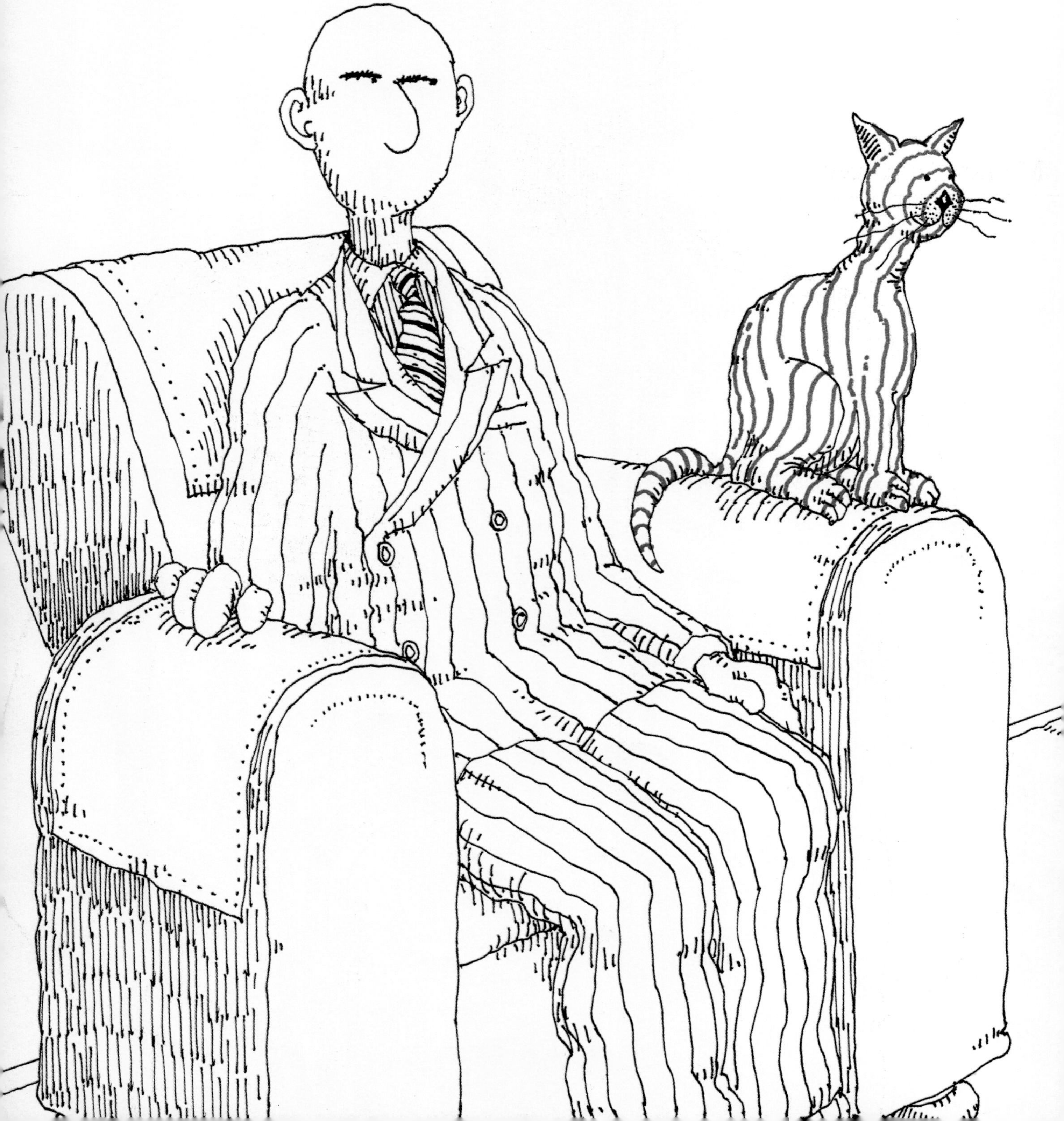

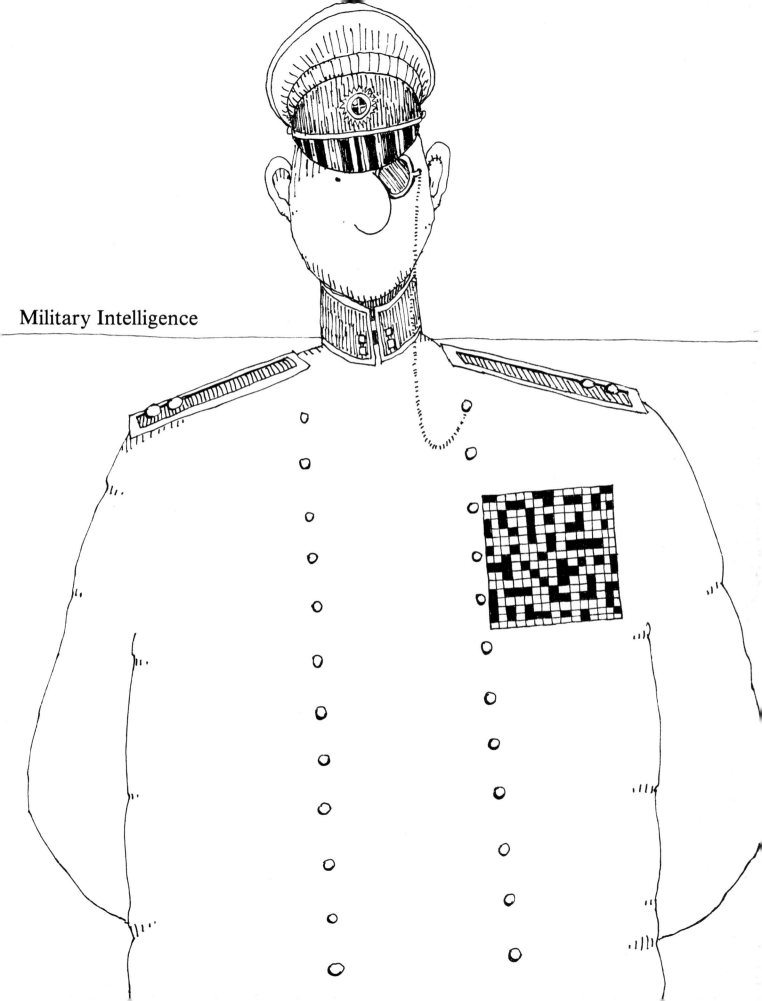

Military Intelligence

Brigadier Ray McDermot
Royal Australian Army Corps

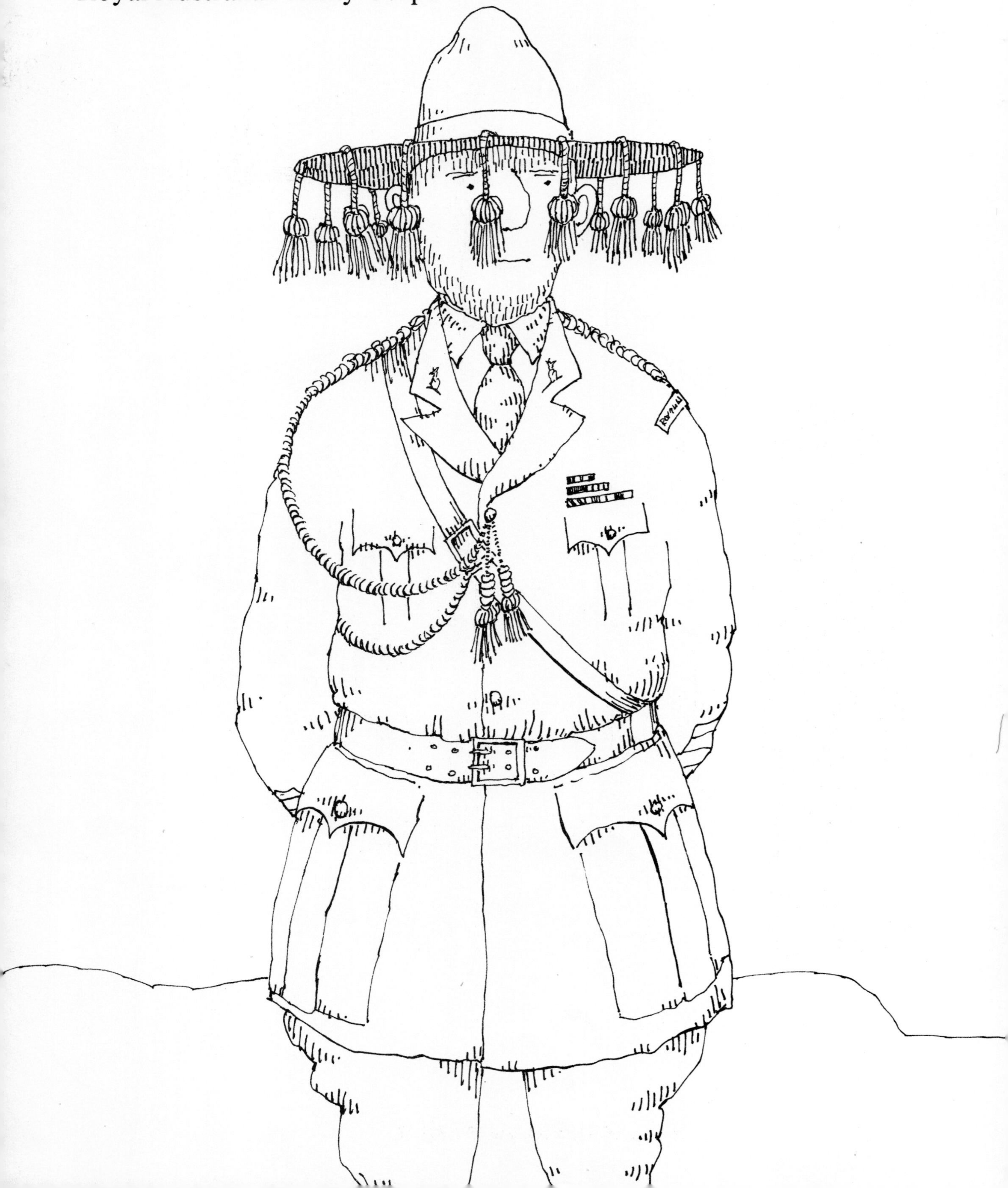

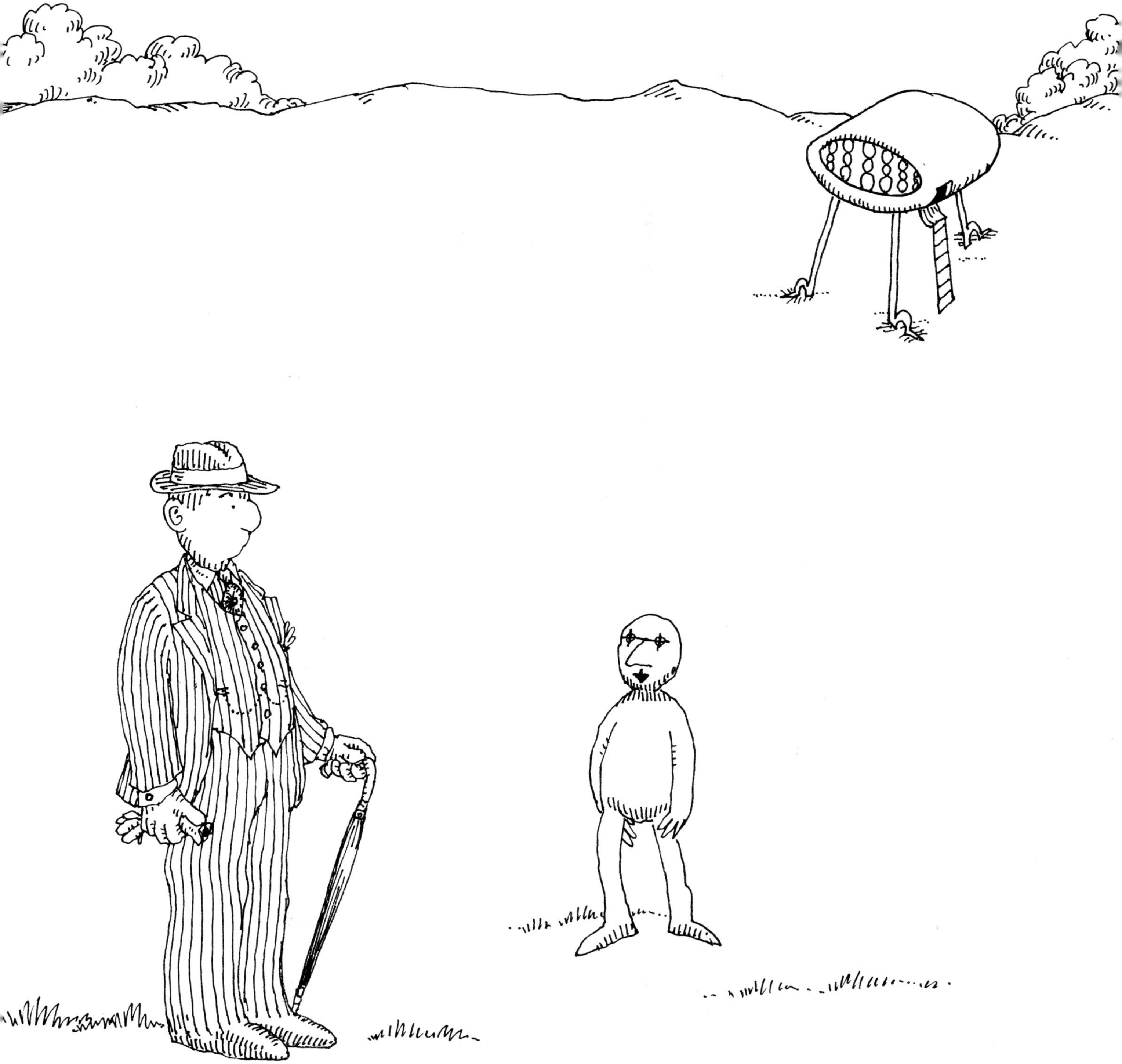

'Take me to your tailor.'

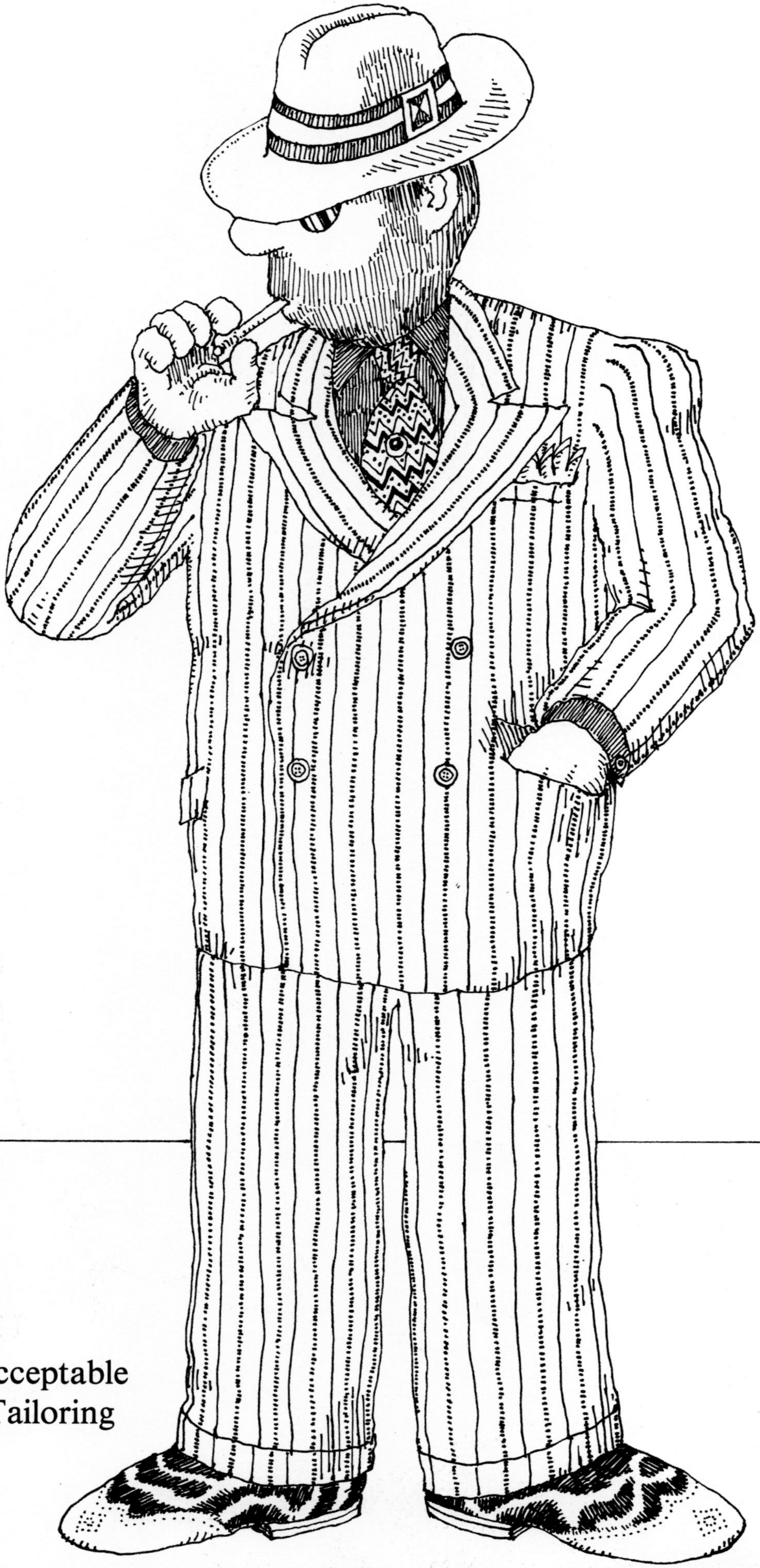

The Unacceptable
Face of Tailoring

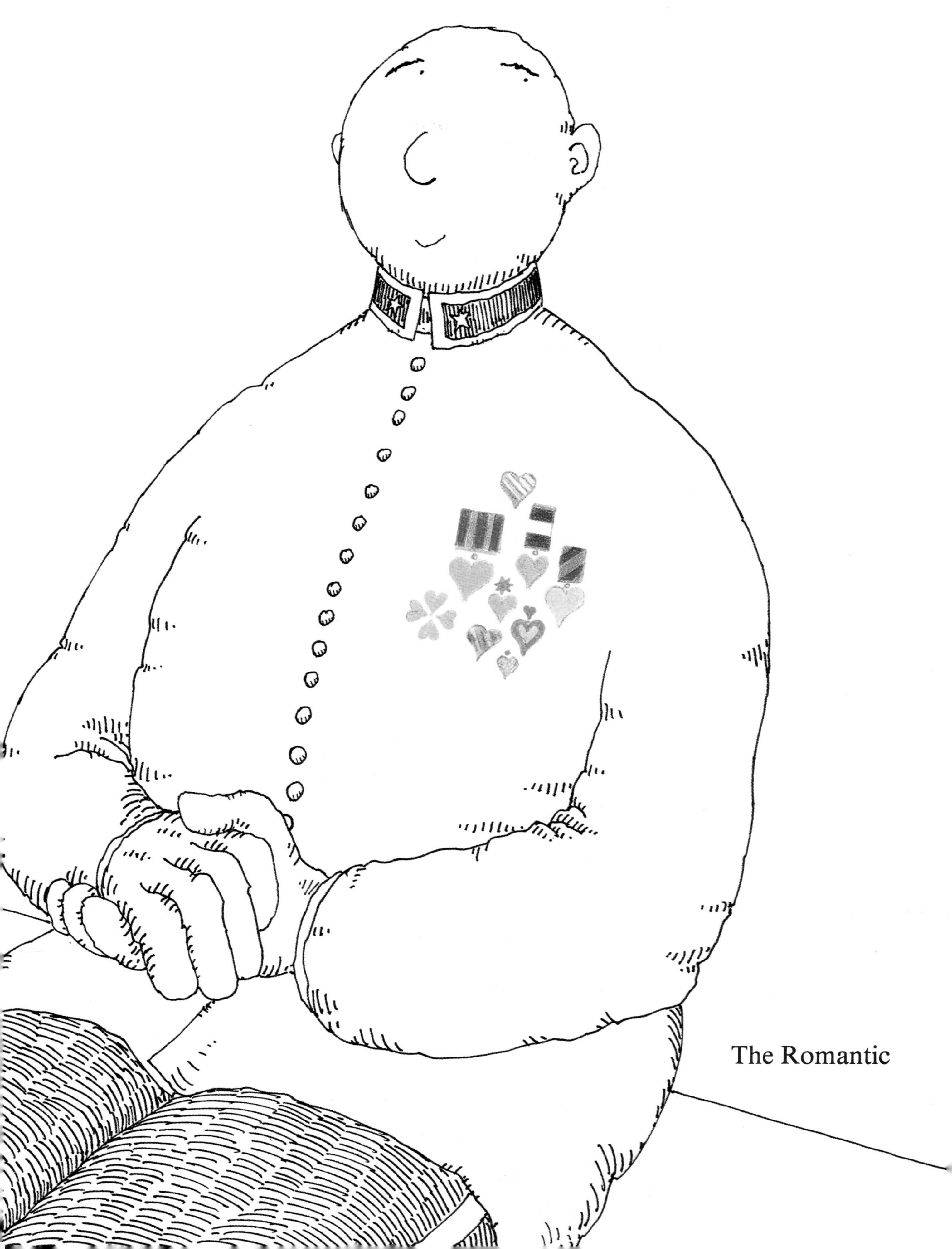

The Romantic

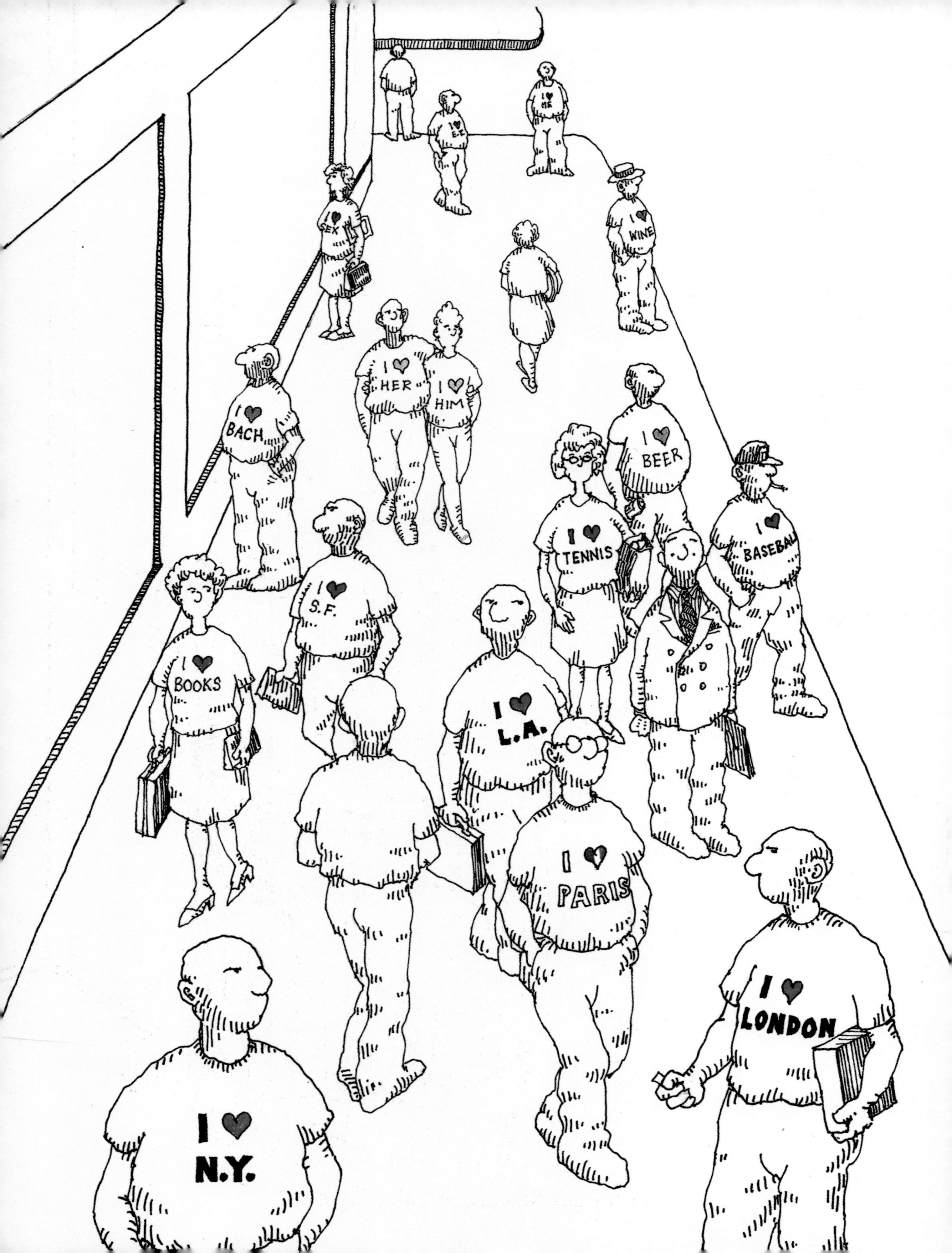
I ♥ E.T.
I ♥ ME
I ♥ SEX
I ♥ WINE
I ♥ HER
I ♥ HIM
I ♥ BACH
I ♥ BEER
I ♥ TENNIS
I ♥ BASEBAL
I ♥ S.F.
I ♥ BOOKS
I ♥ L.A.
I ♥ PARIS
I ♥ LONDON
I ♥ N.Y.

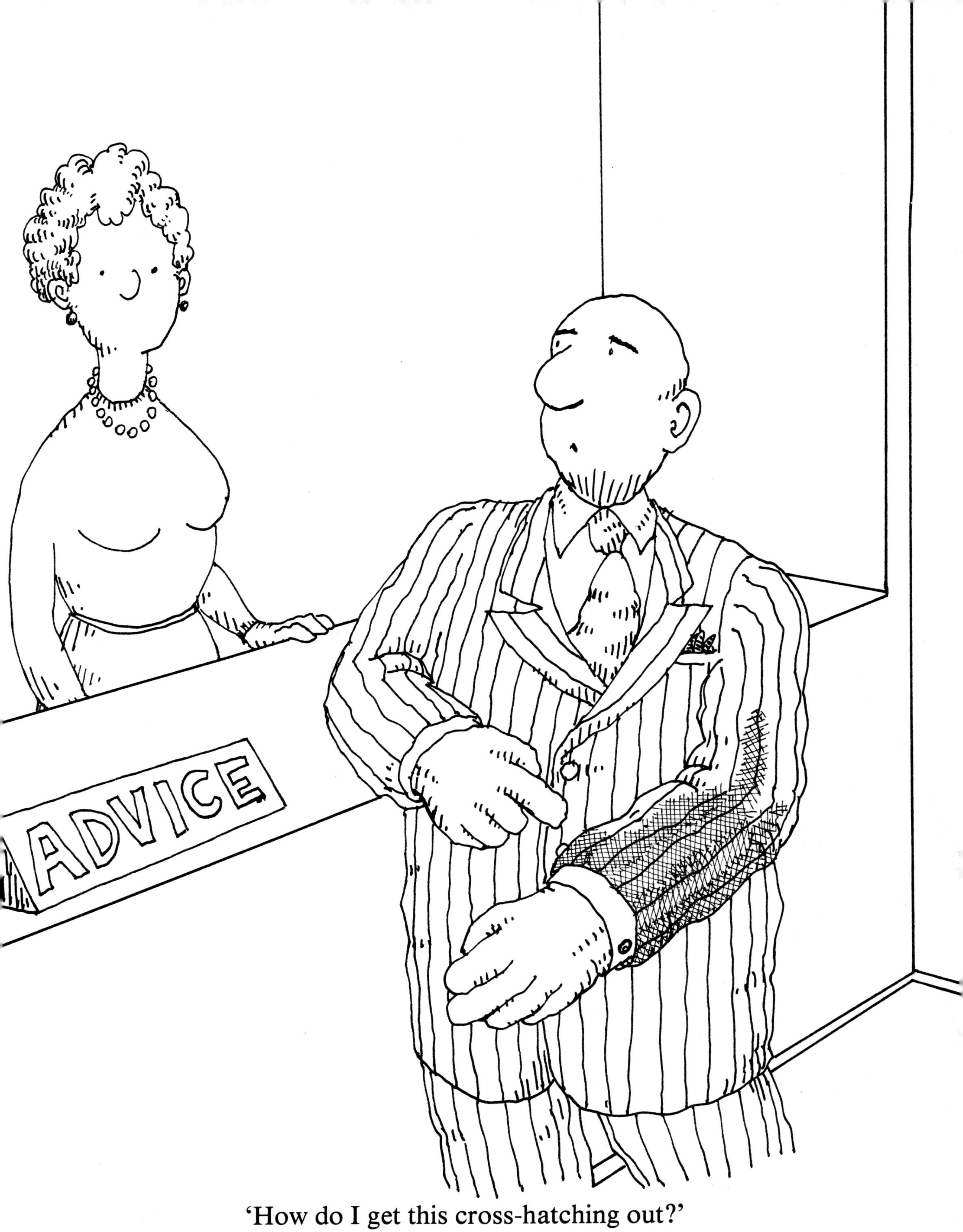
ADVICE

'How do I get this cross-hatching out?'

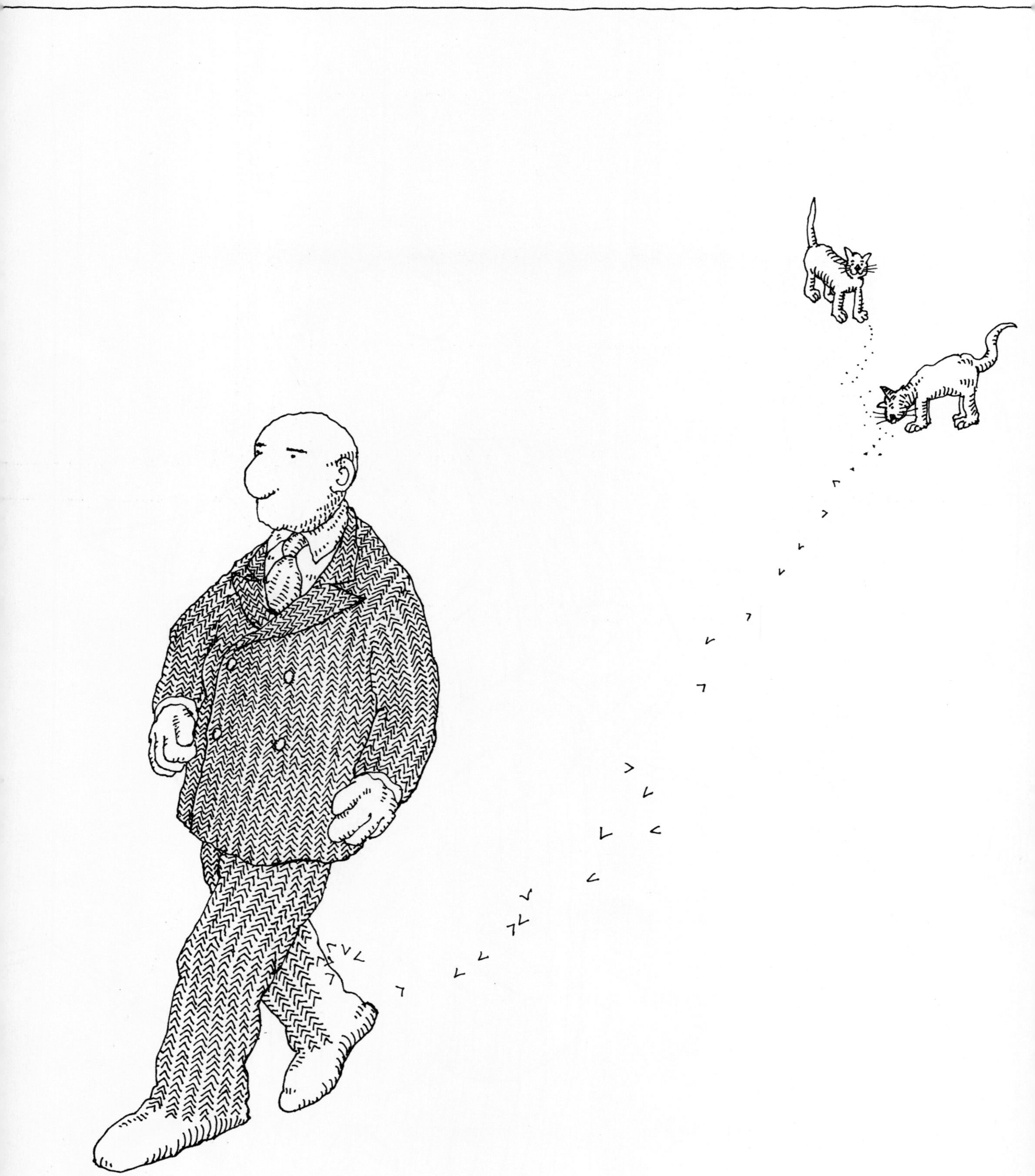

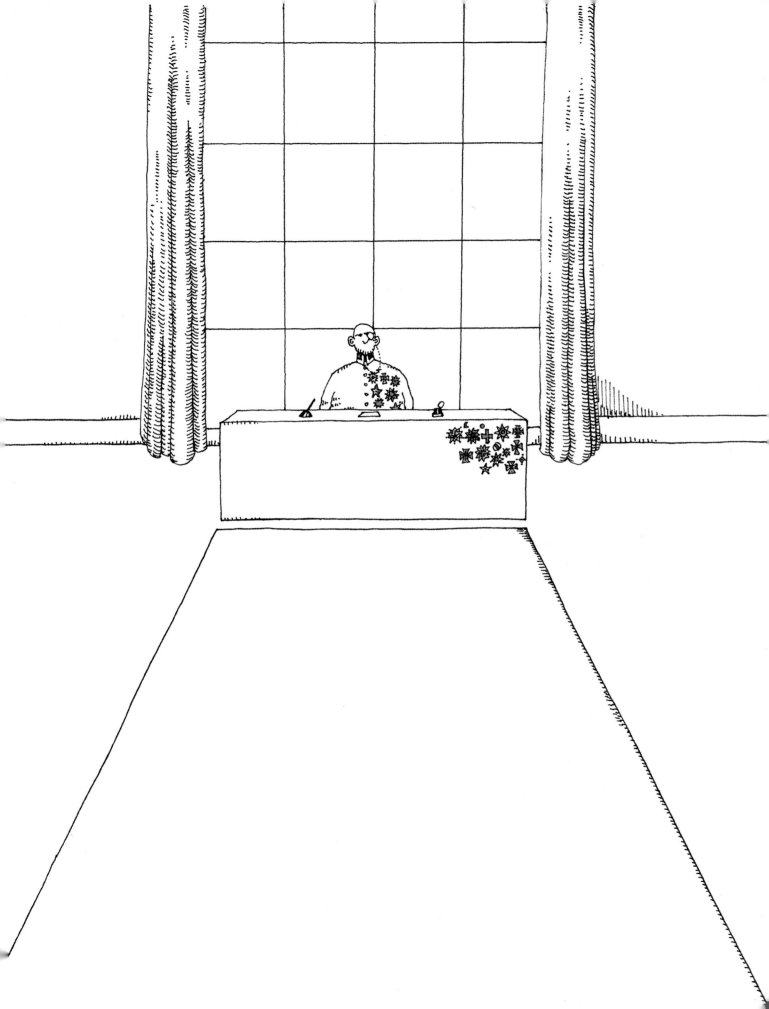

Eldon Furse
Cattle Baron
and
Flag Waver

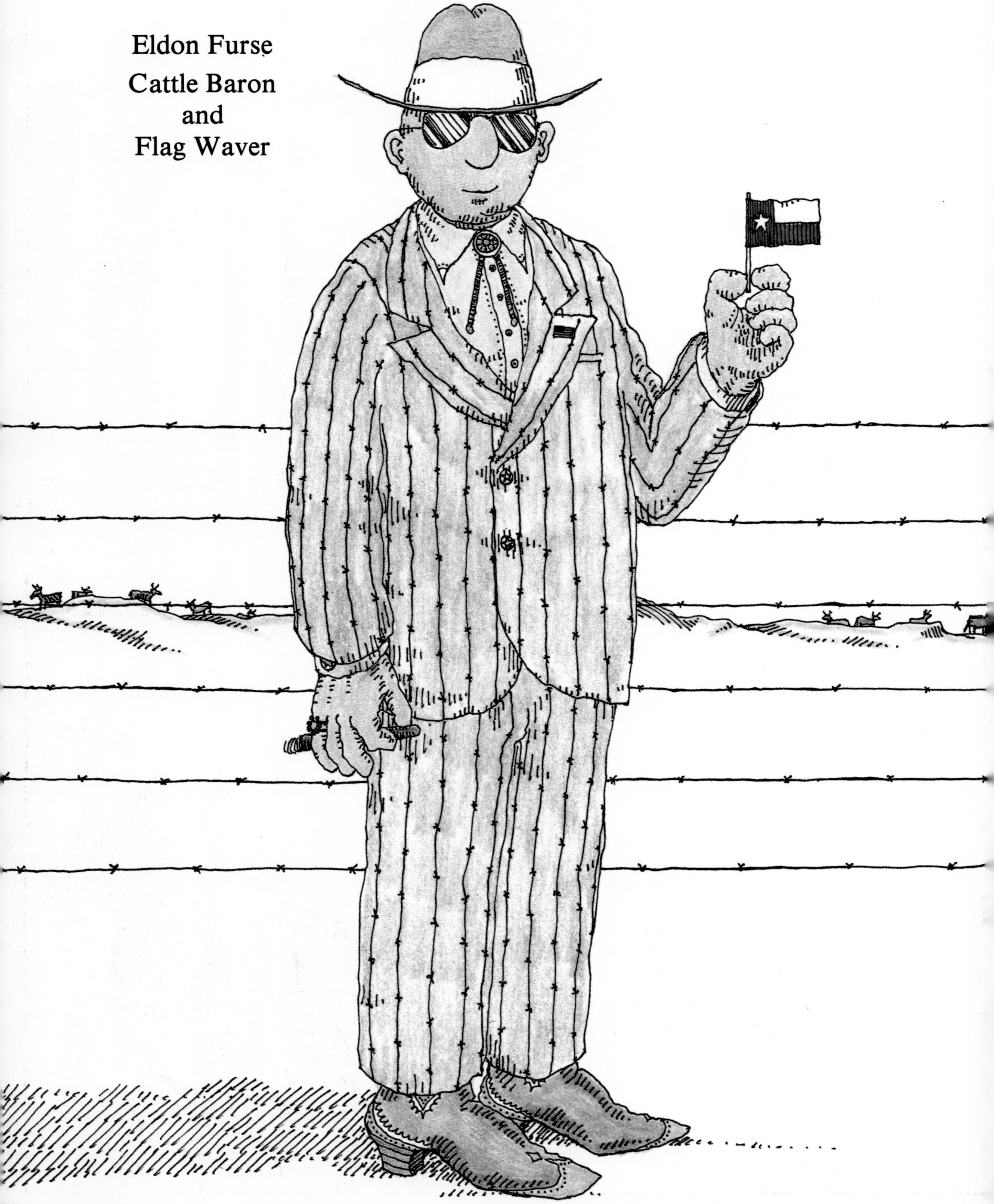

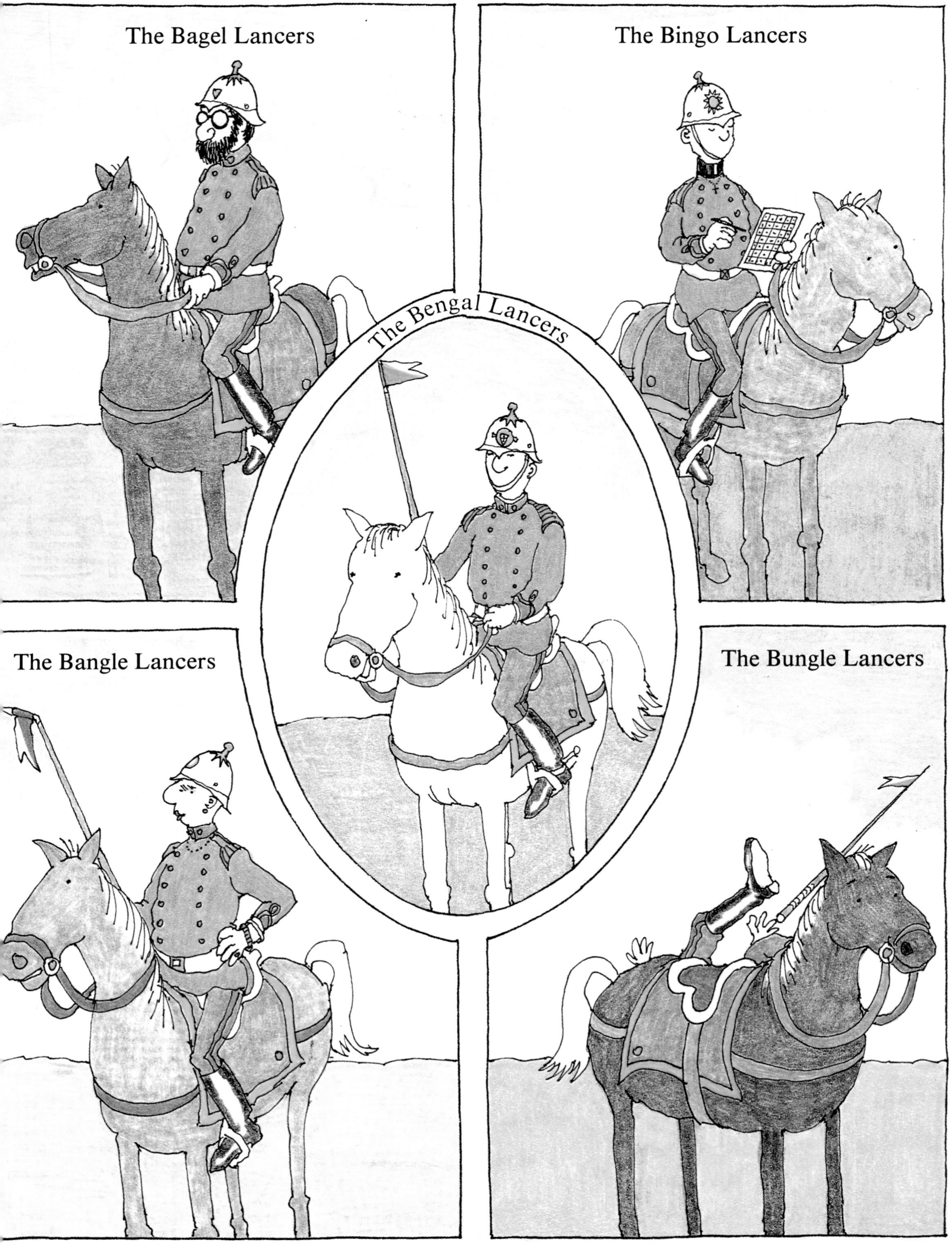
The Bagel Lancers
The Bingo Lancers
The Bengal Lancers
The Bangle Lancers
The Bungle Lancers

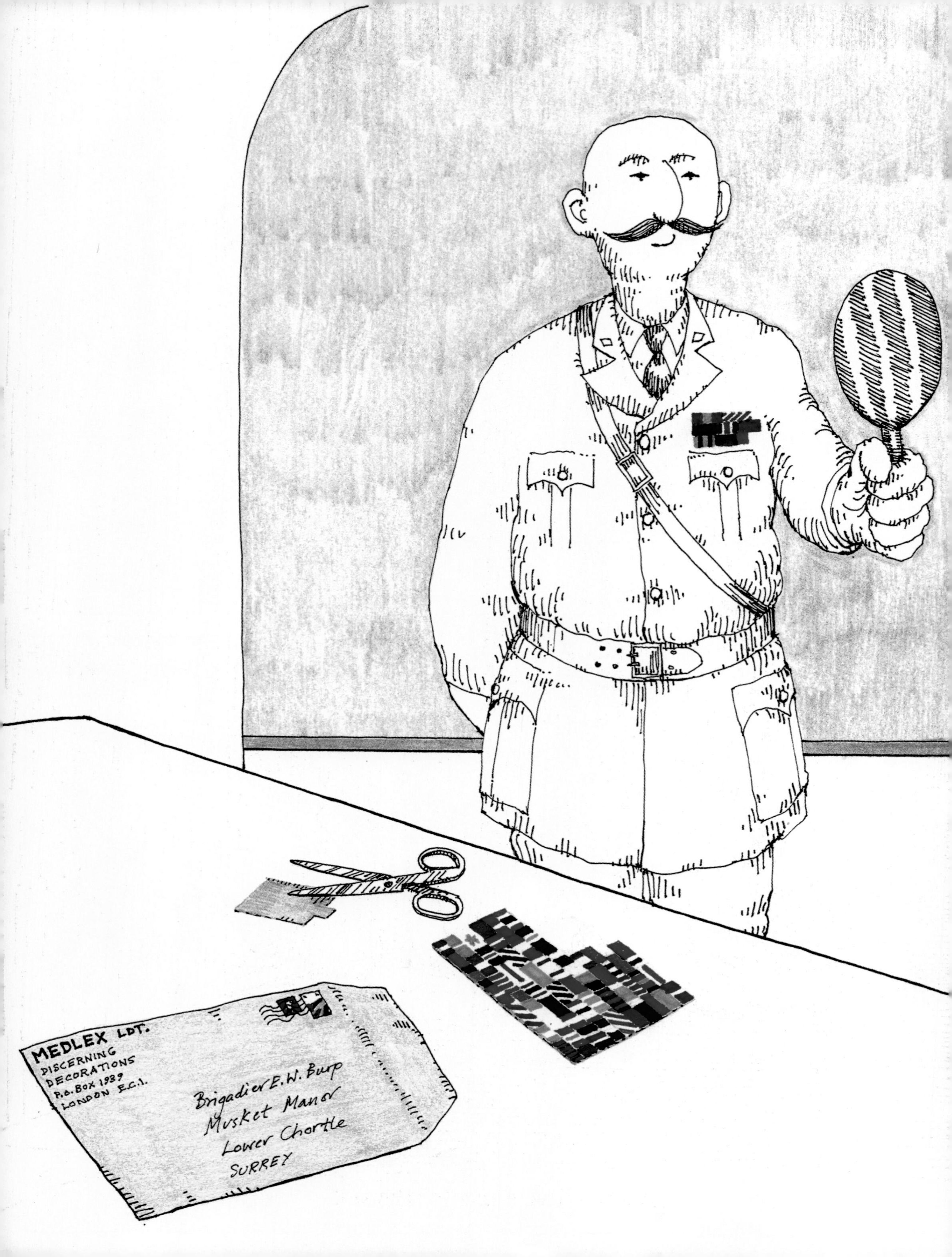
MEDLEX LDT.
DISCERNING
DECORATIONS
P.O. BOX 1939
LONDON E.C.1.
Brigadier E.W. Burp
Musket Manor
Lower Chortle
SURREY

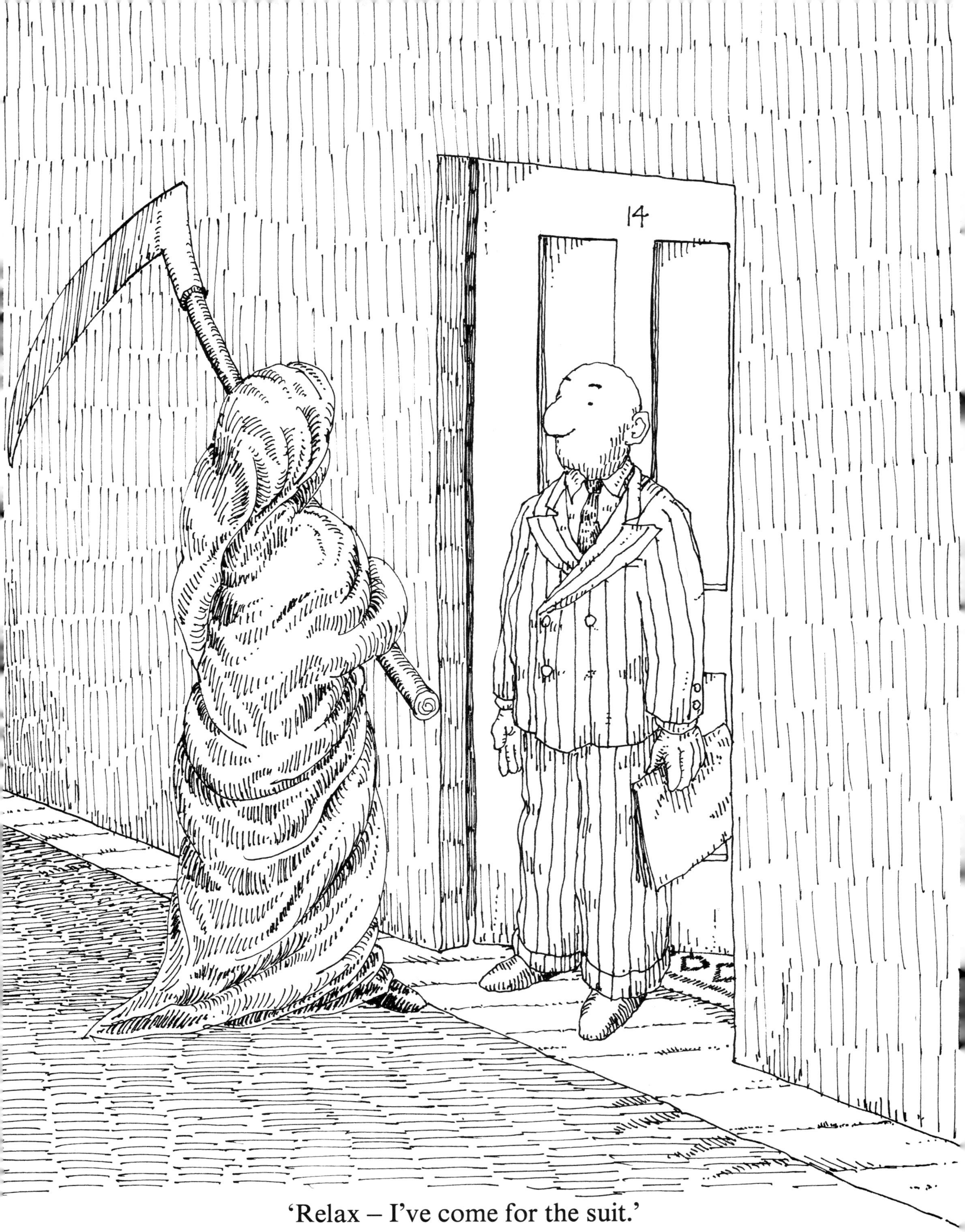
14

‘Relax – I’ve come for the suit.’

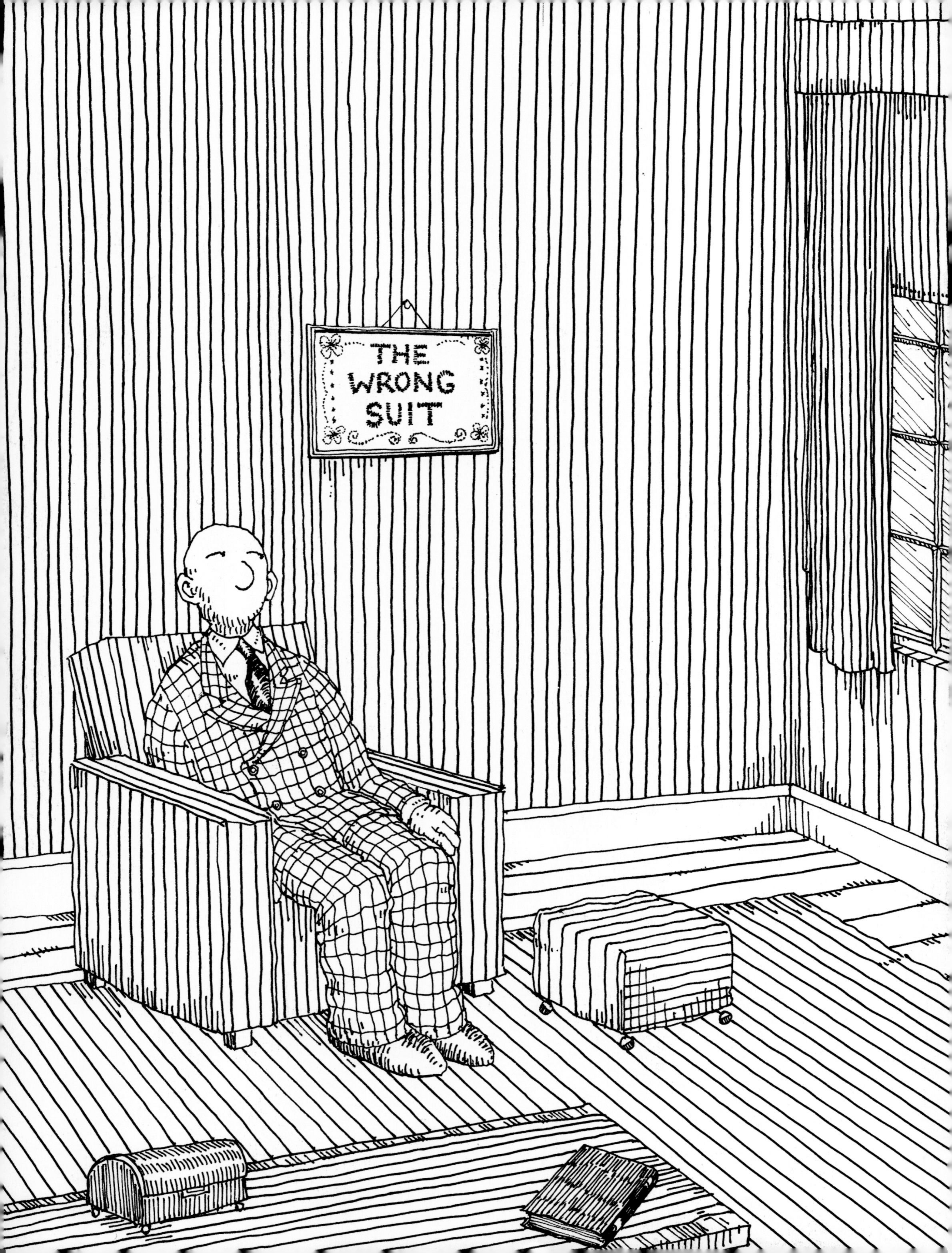
THE
WRONG
SUIT

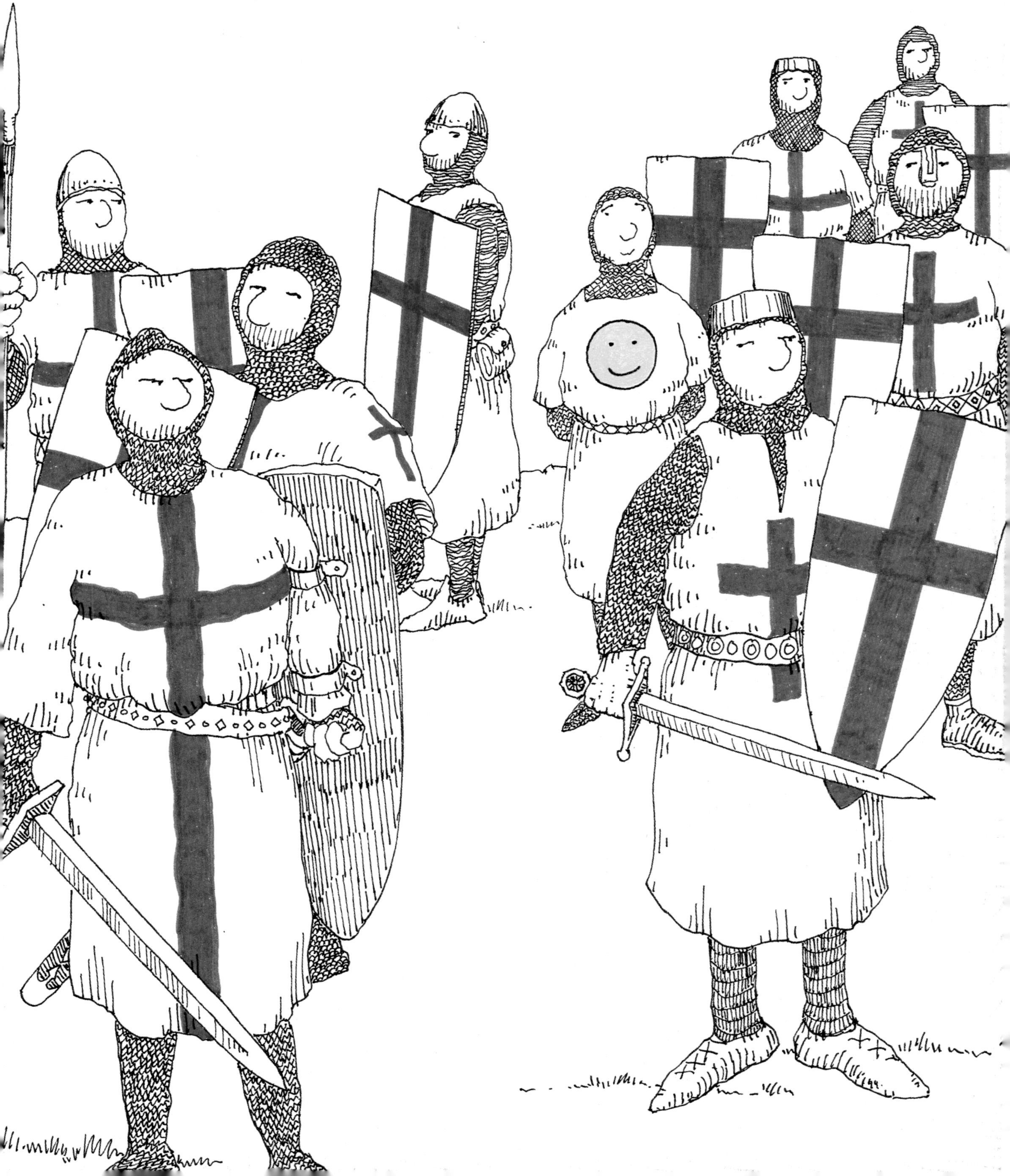

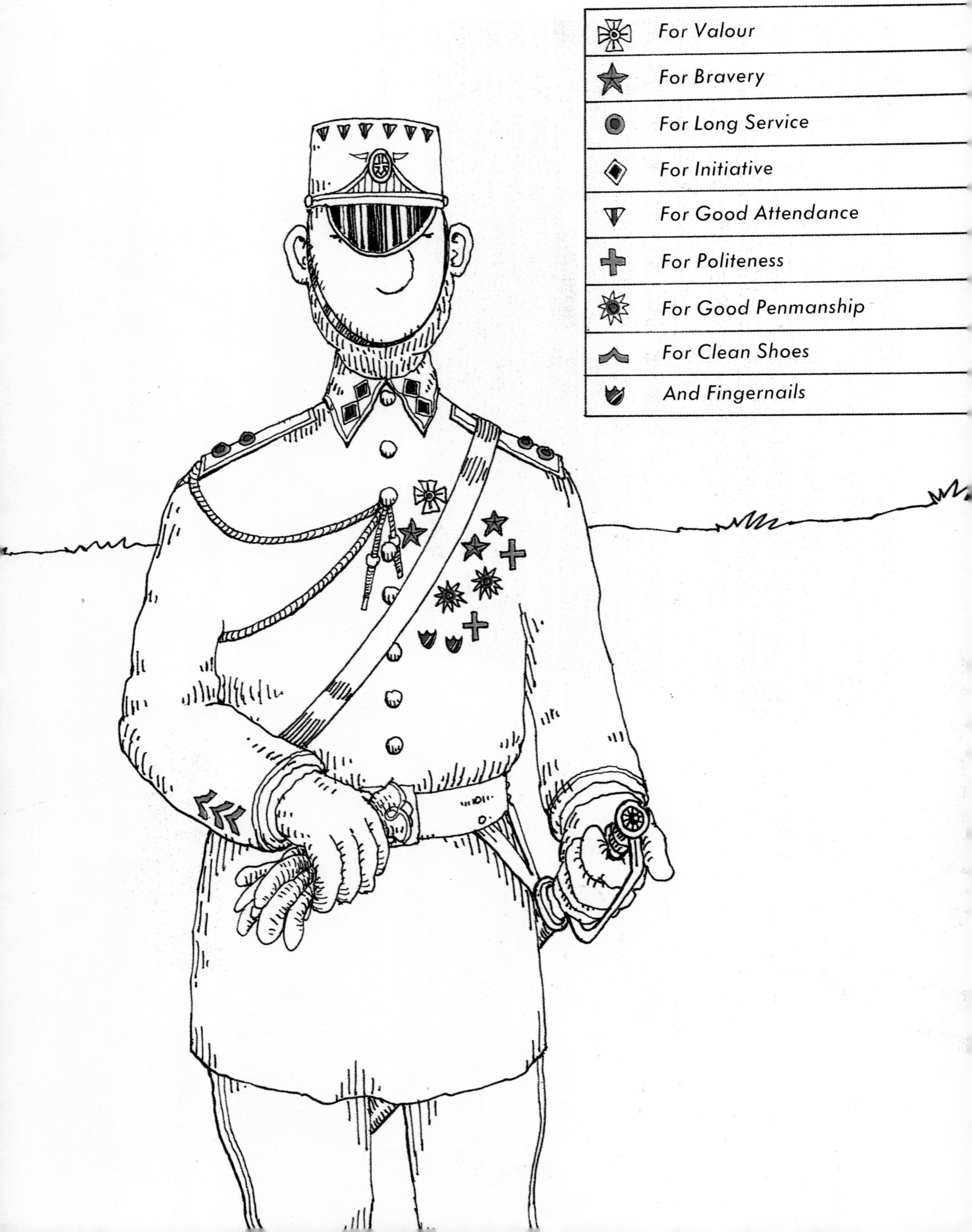
For Valour
For Bravery
For Long Service
For Initiative
For Good Attendance
For Politeness
For Good Penmanship
For Clean Shoes
And Fingernails

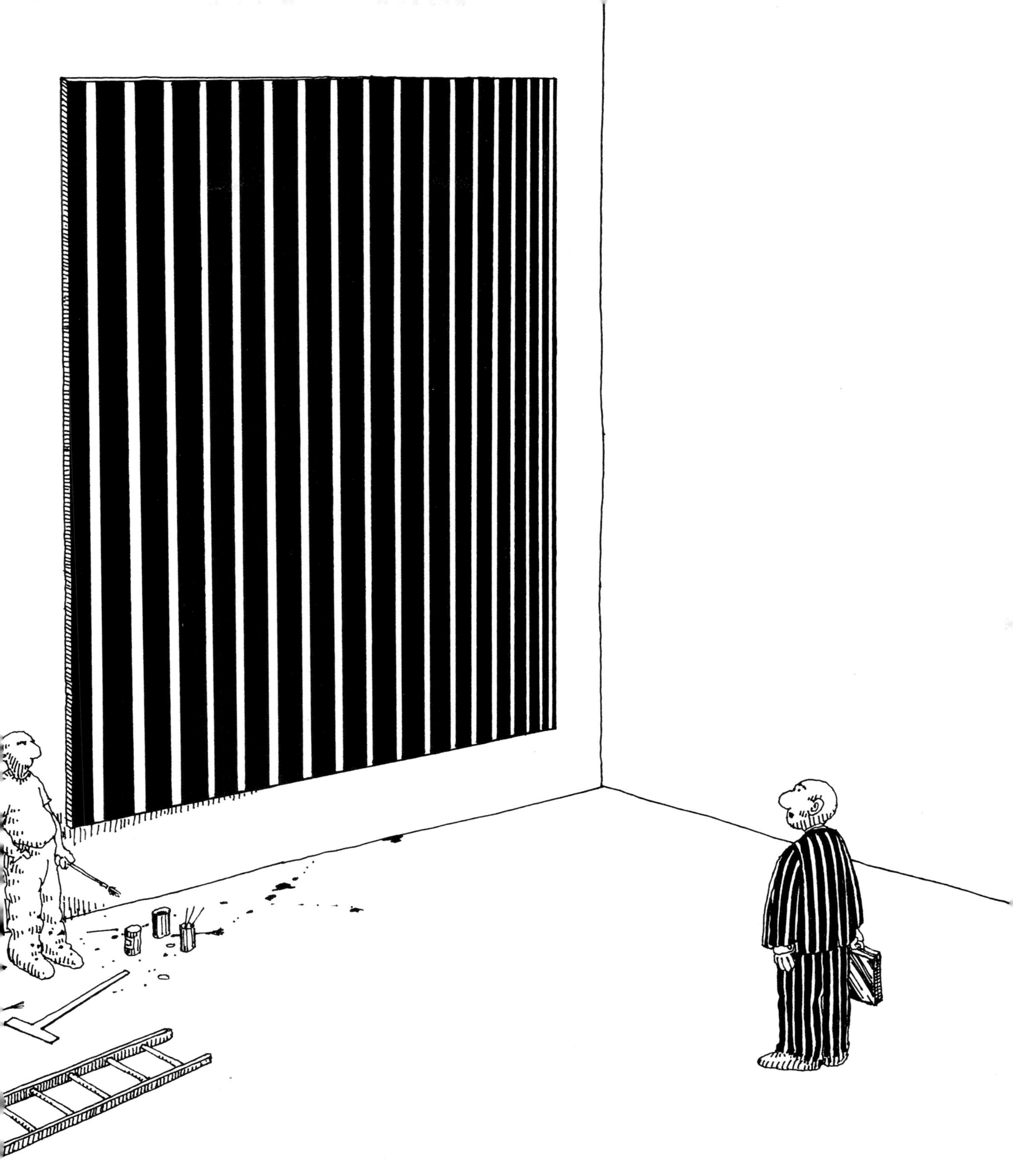

'I love it!'

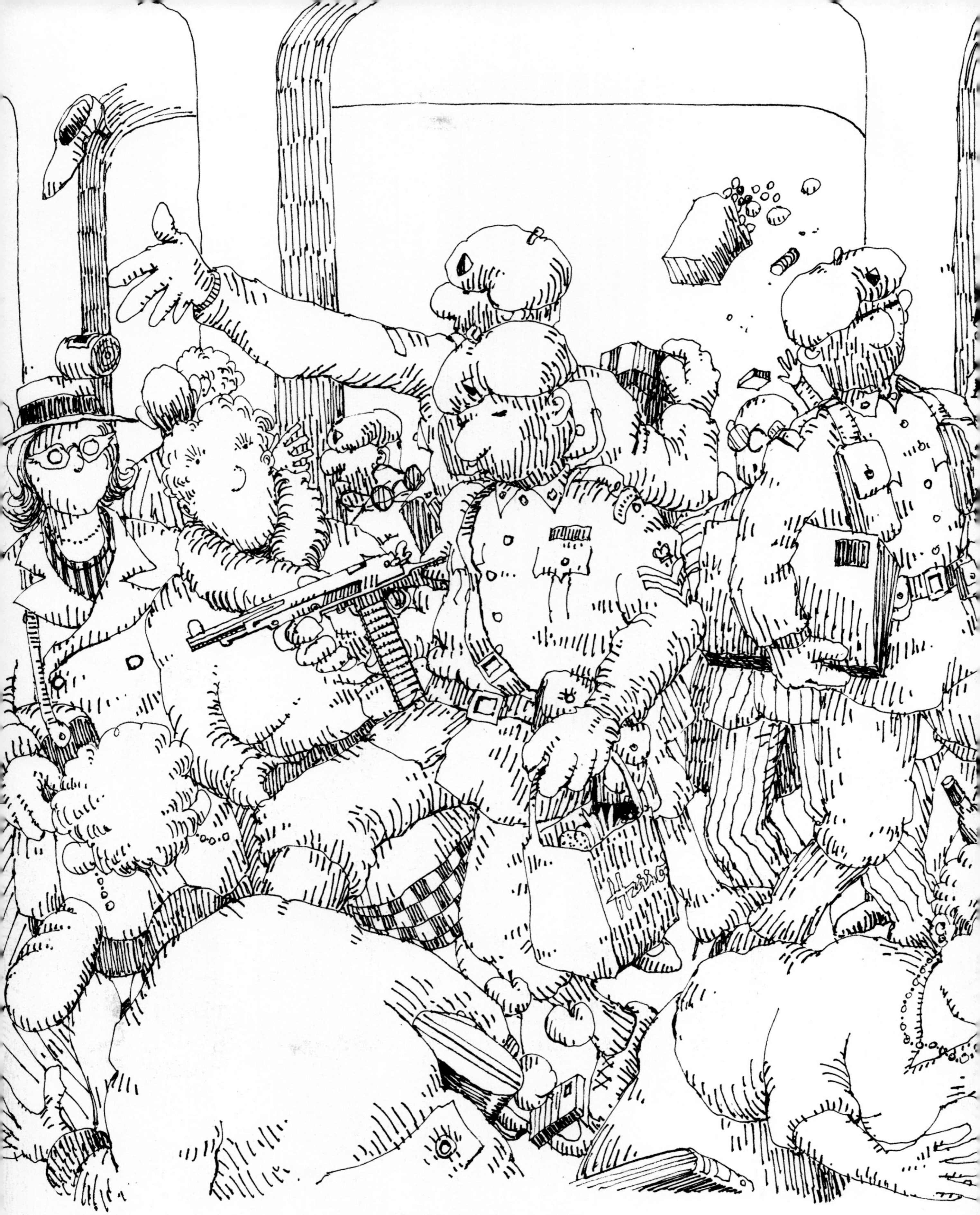

The Commandos Go Shopping

Generalissimo Jesus Delgado Mañana
Director De La Burocracia Gubernamental de Mexico

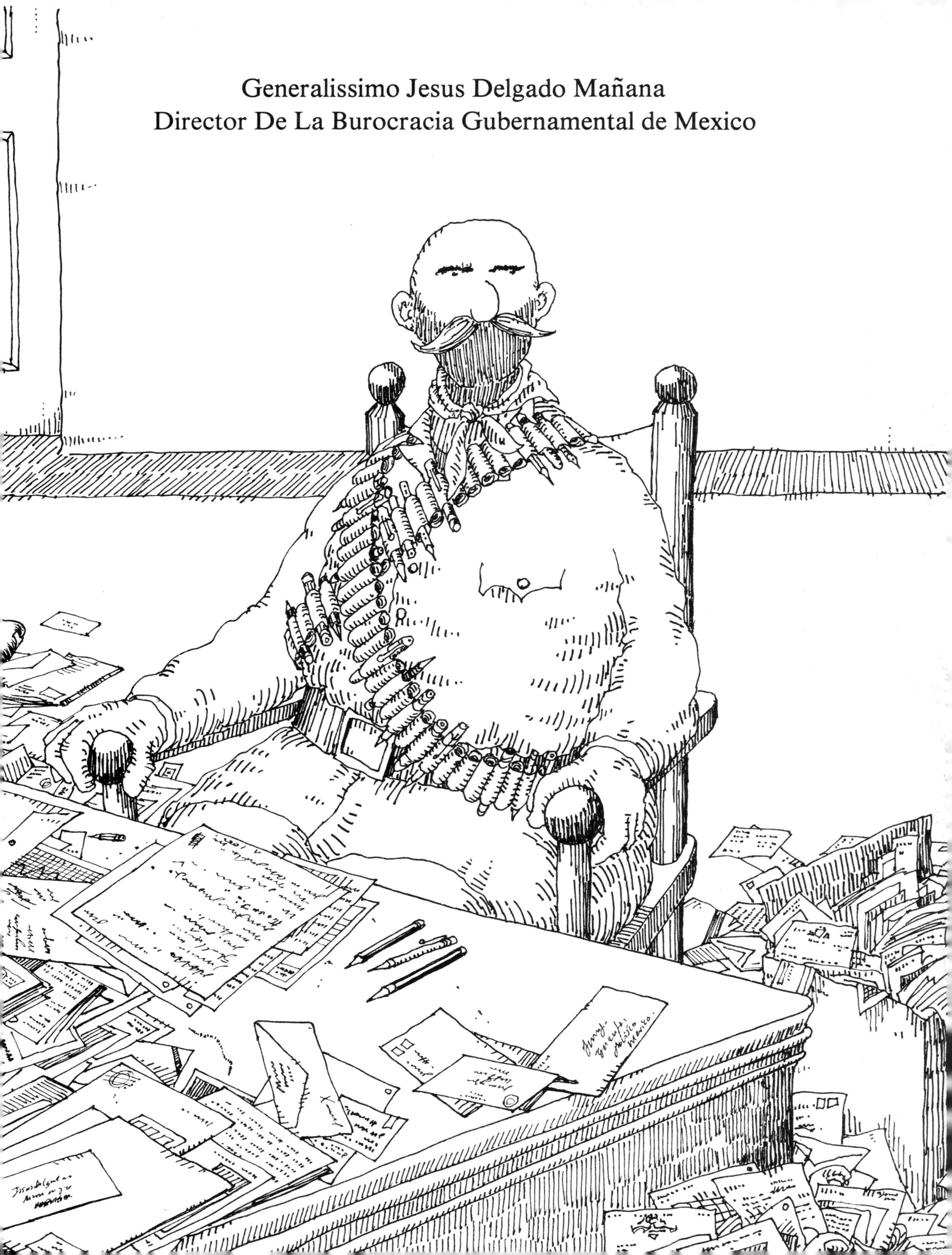

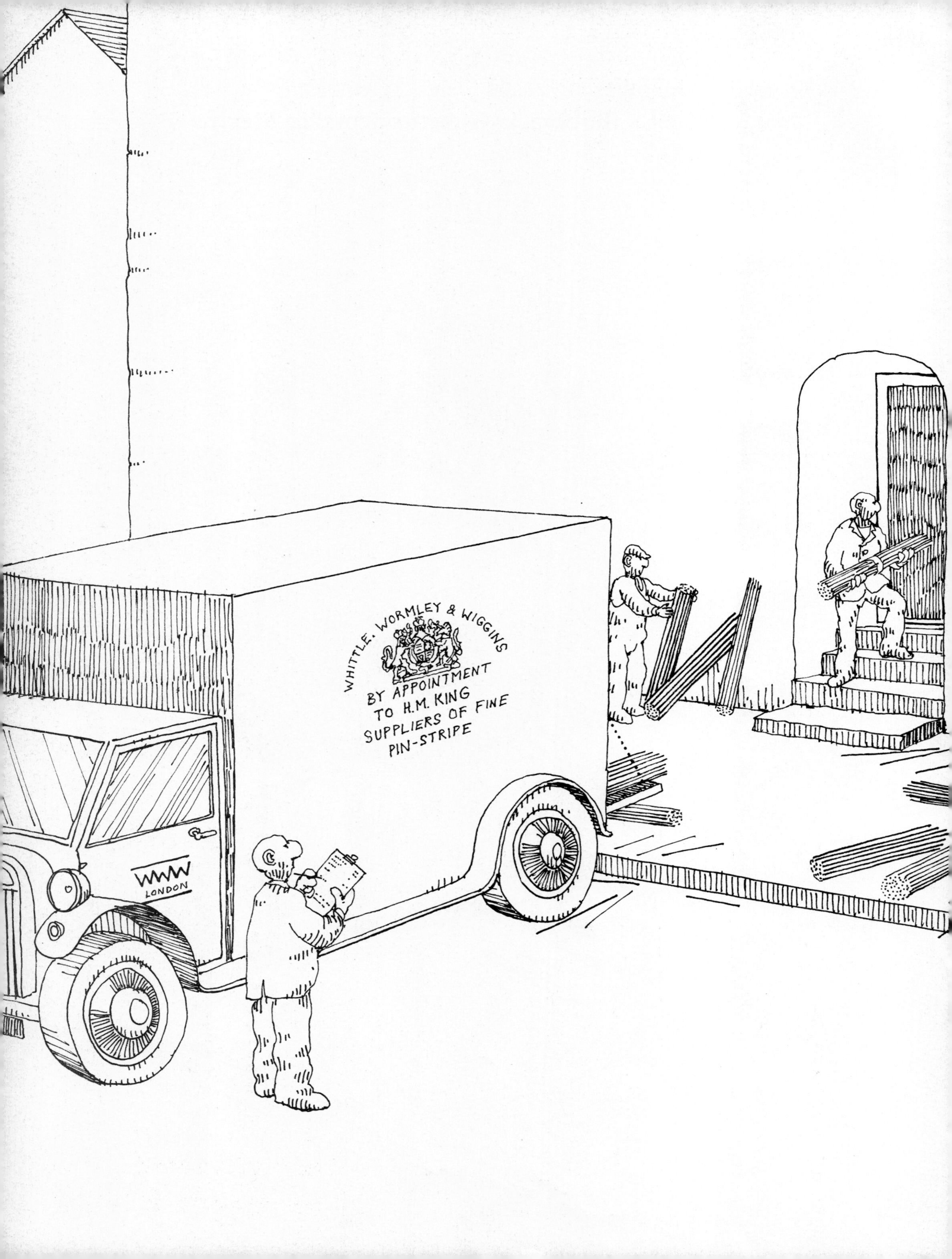
WHITTLE, WORMLEY & WIGGINS
BY APPOINTMENT
TO H.M. KING
SUPPLIERS OF FINE
PIN-STRIPE
WWW
LONDON

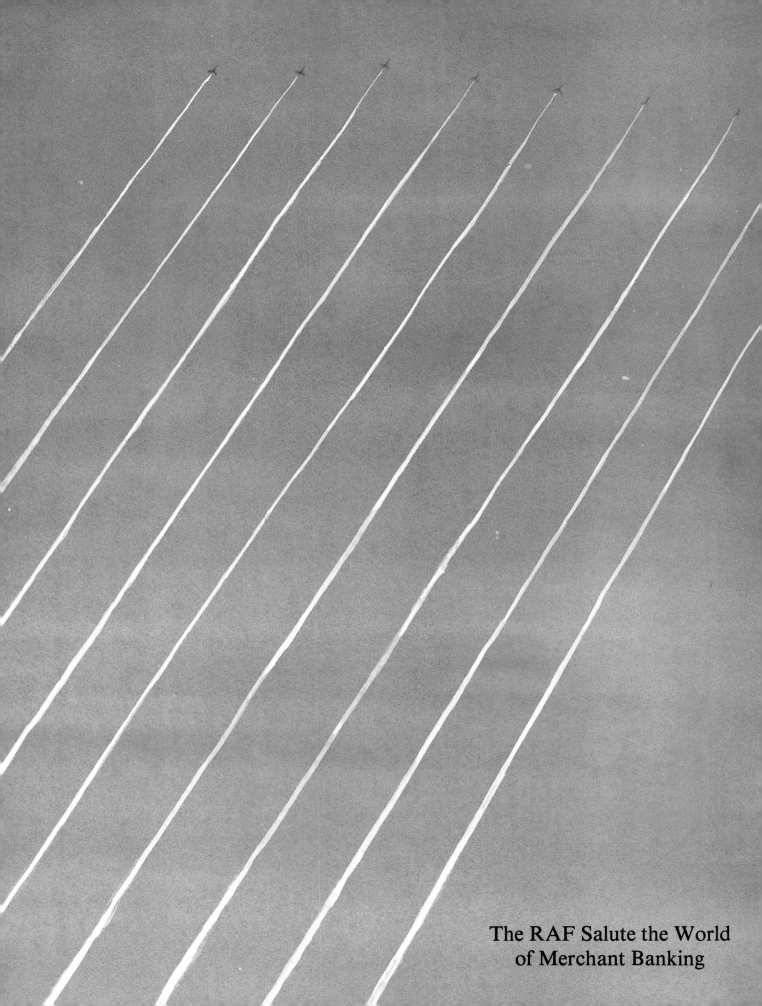

The RAF Salute the World
of Merchant Banking

Robin Hood and his Merry Men

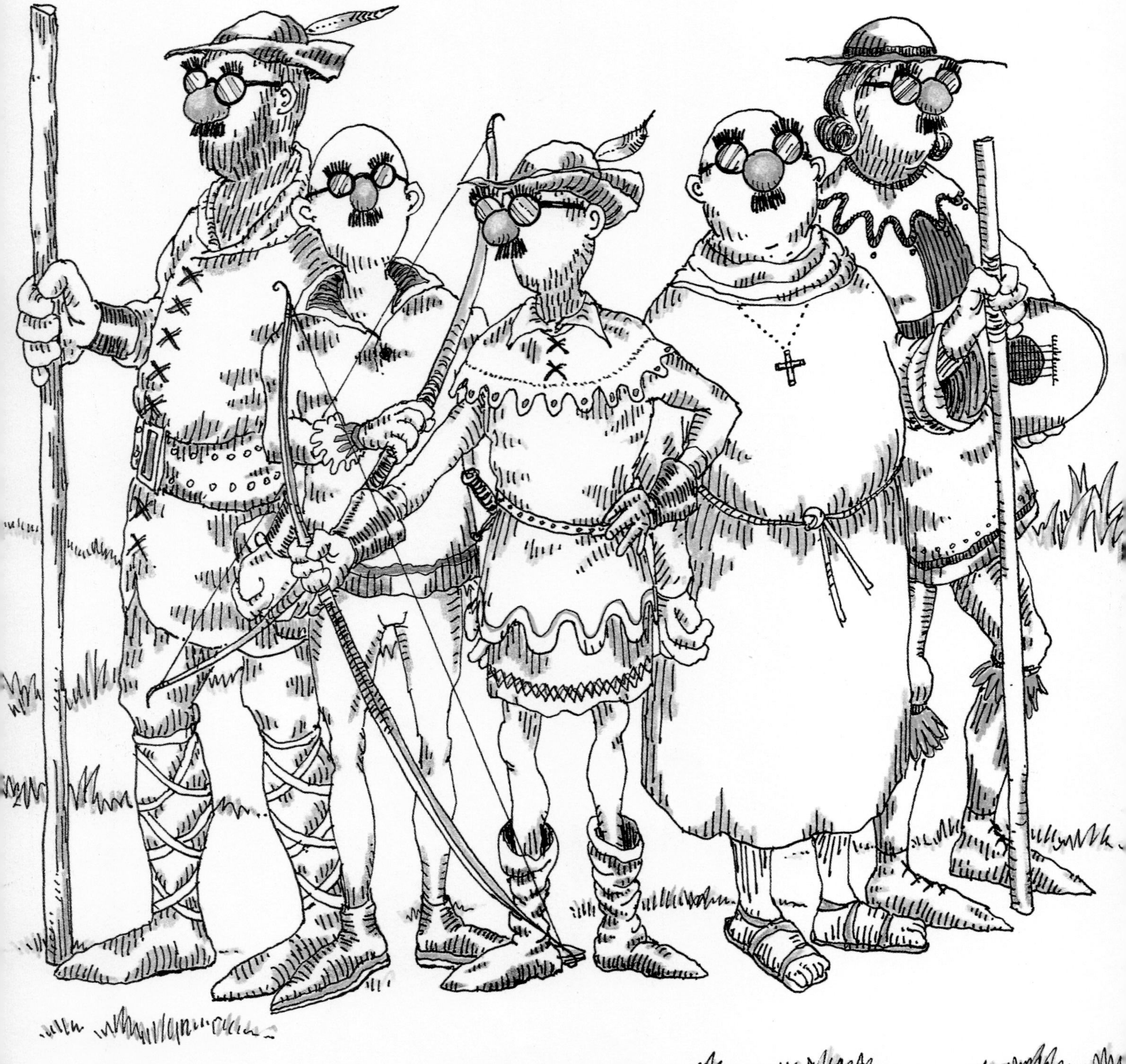

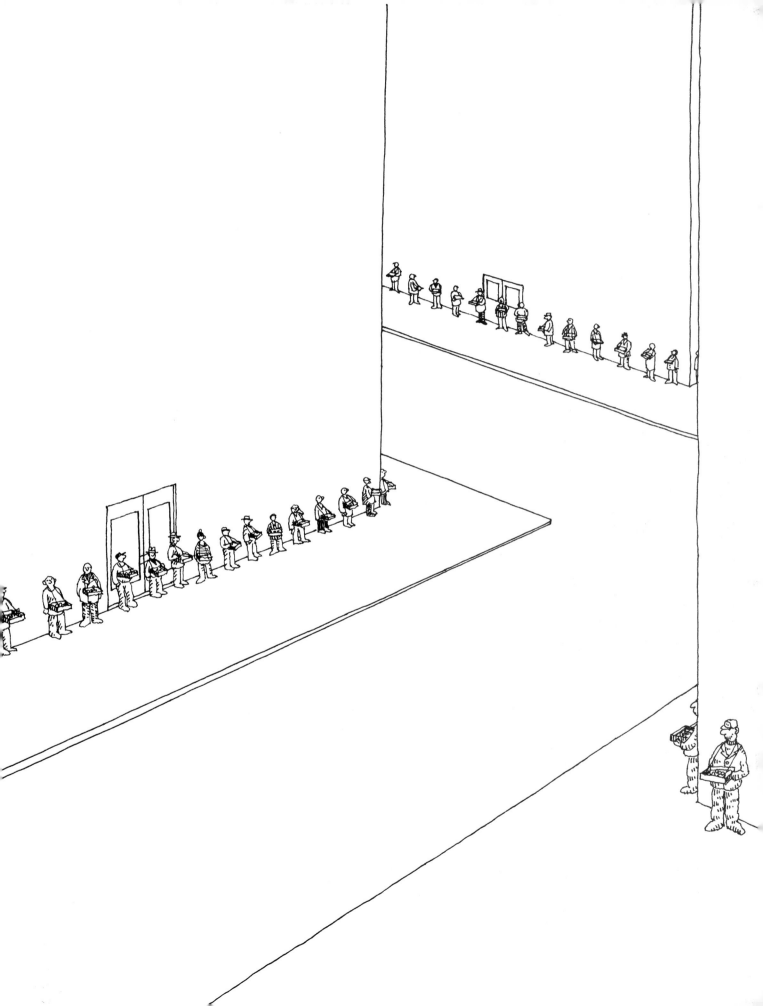

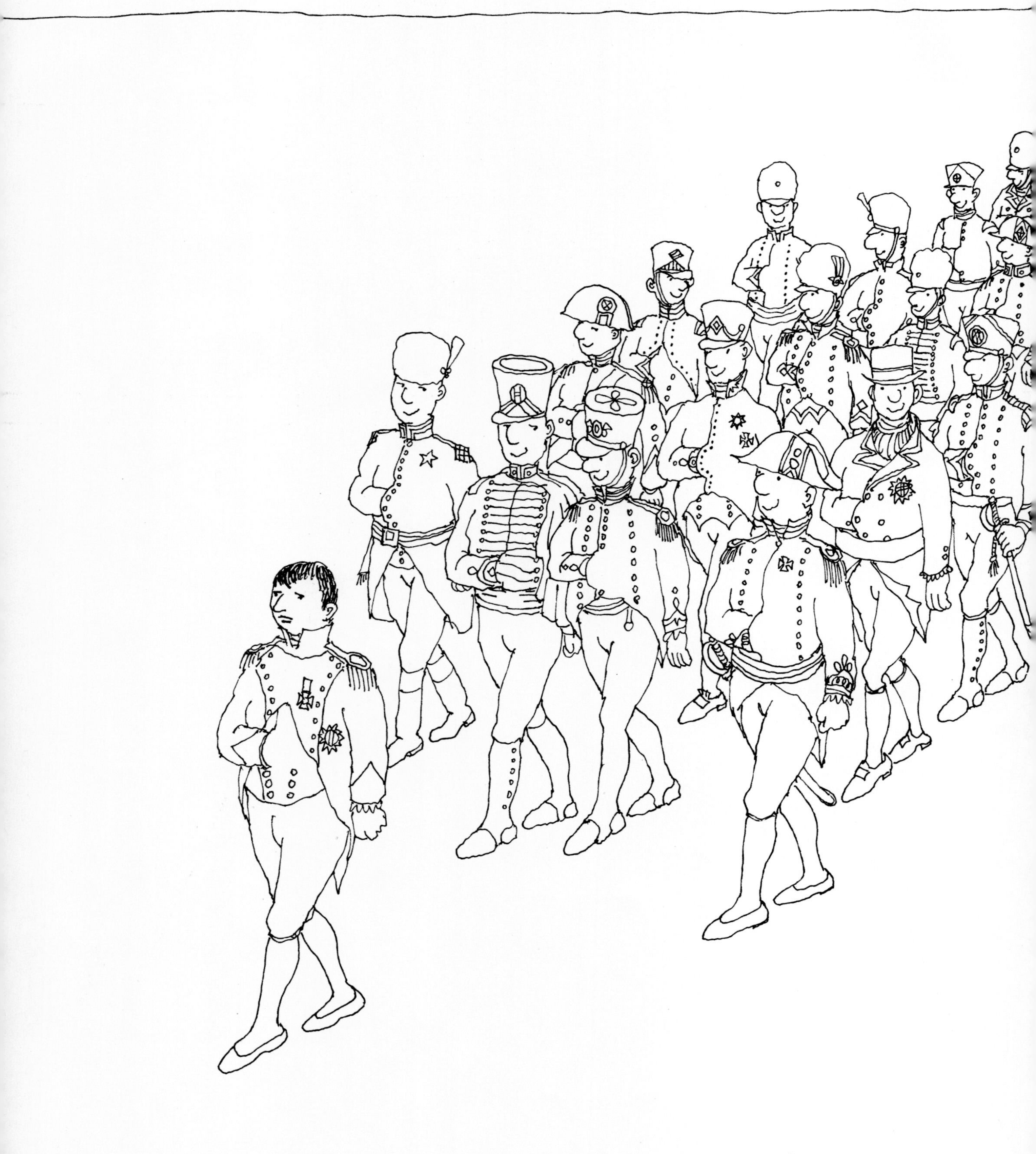

Se Moquer de Lui

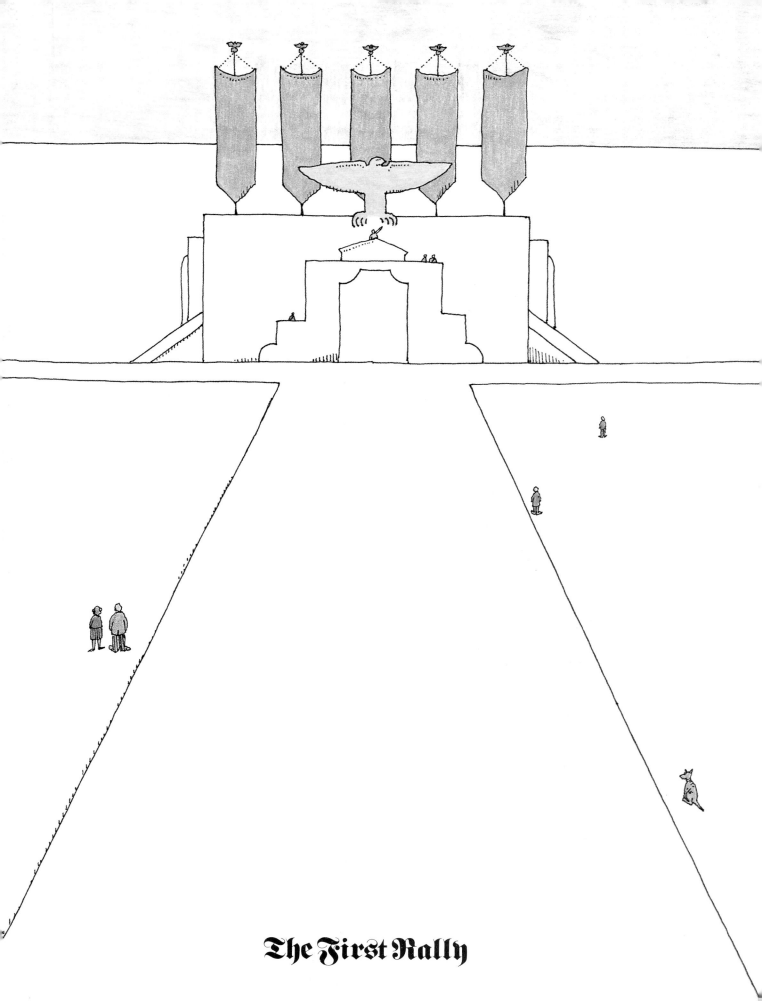

The First Rally

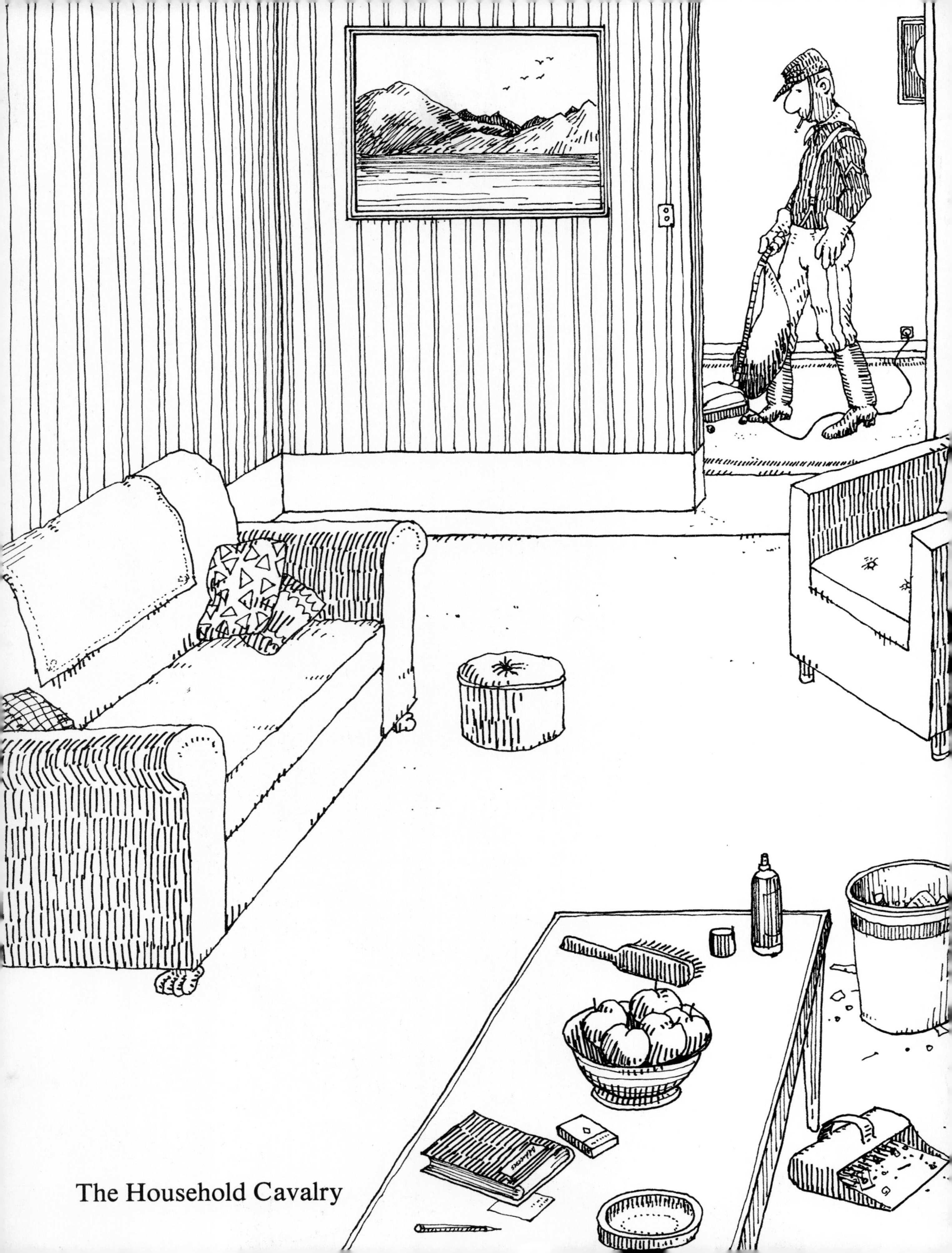

The Household Cavalry

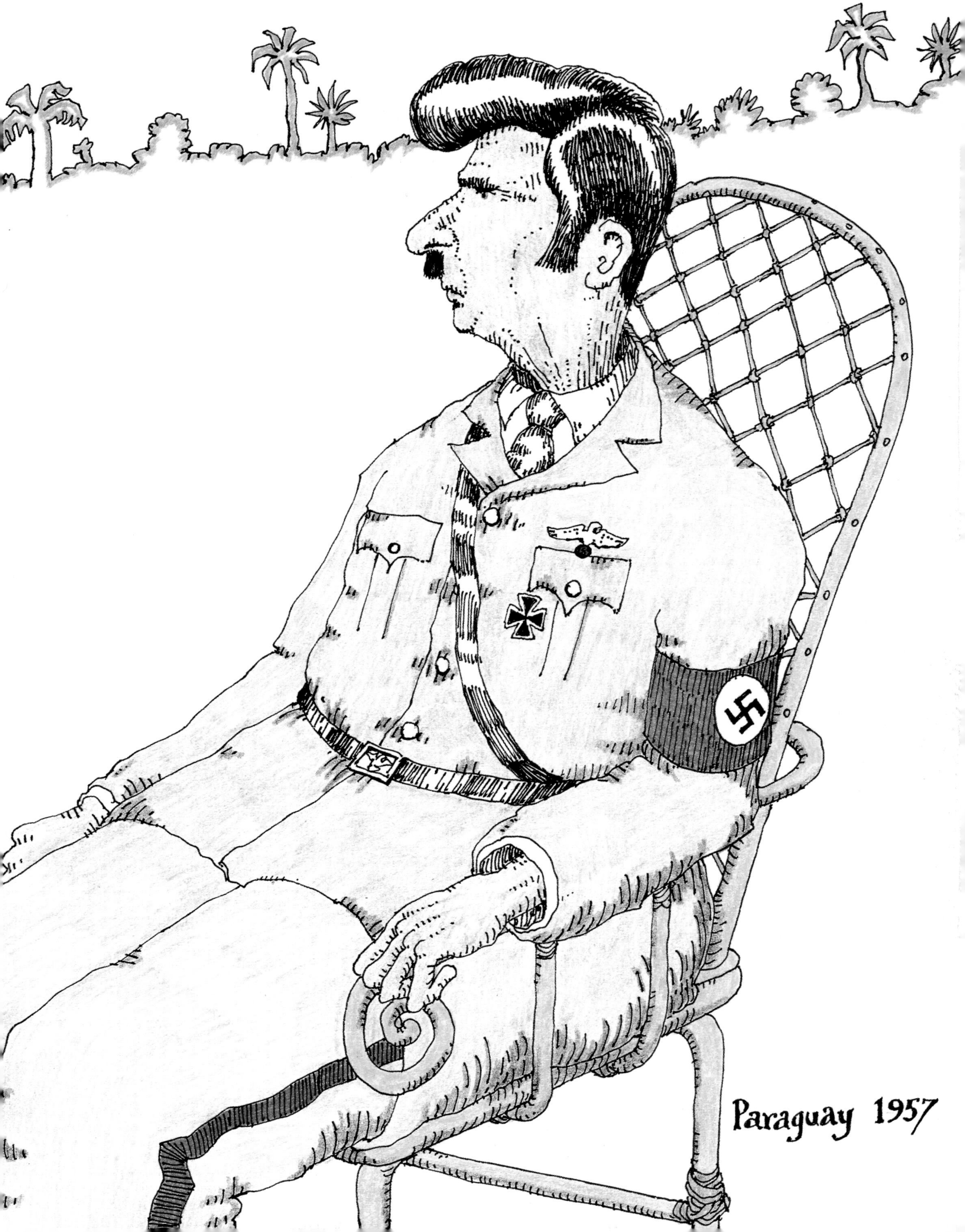

Paraguay 1957

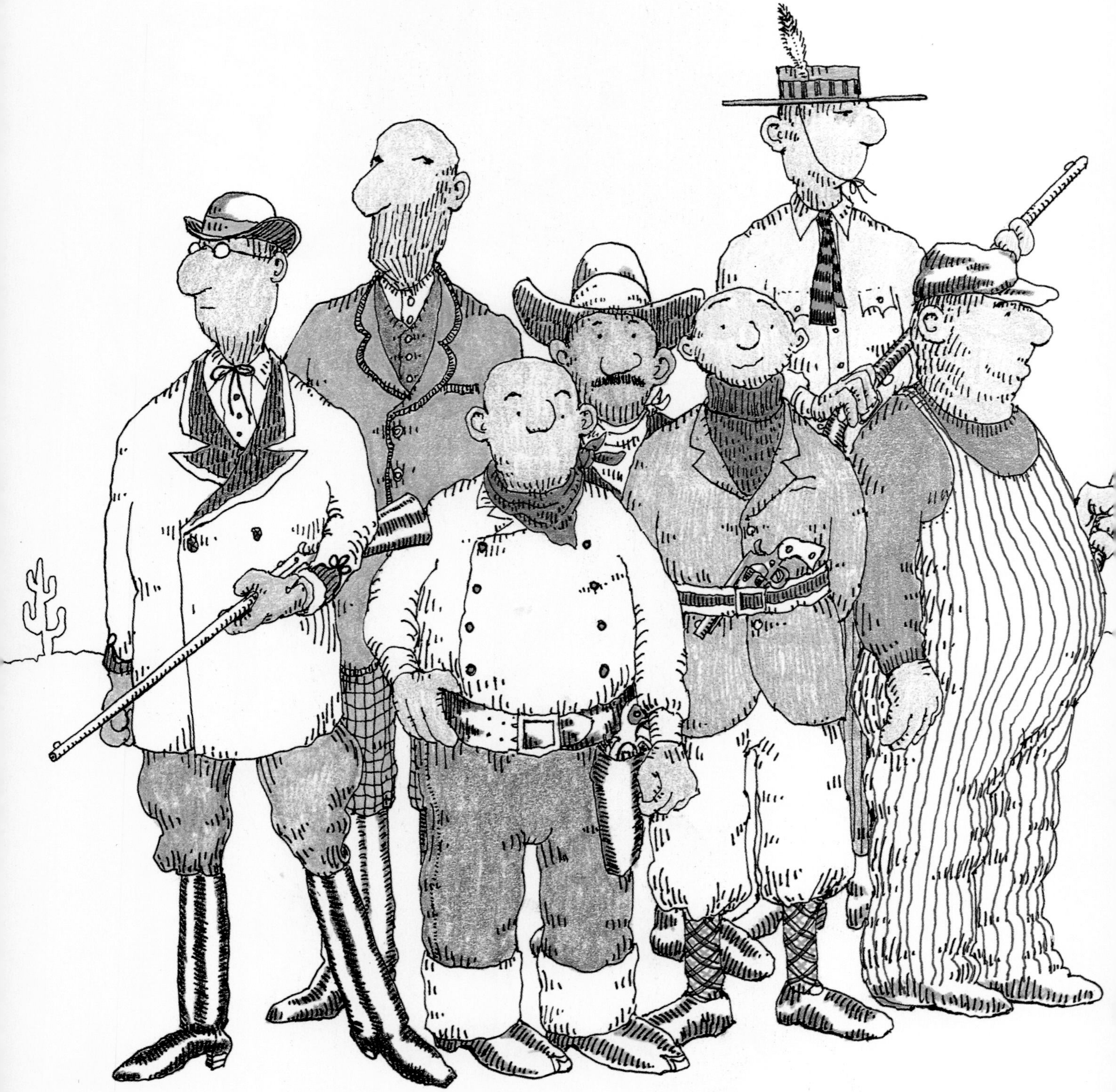

The Magnificent Seven II

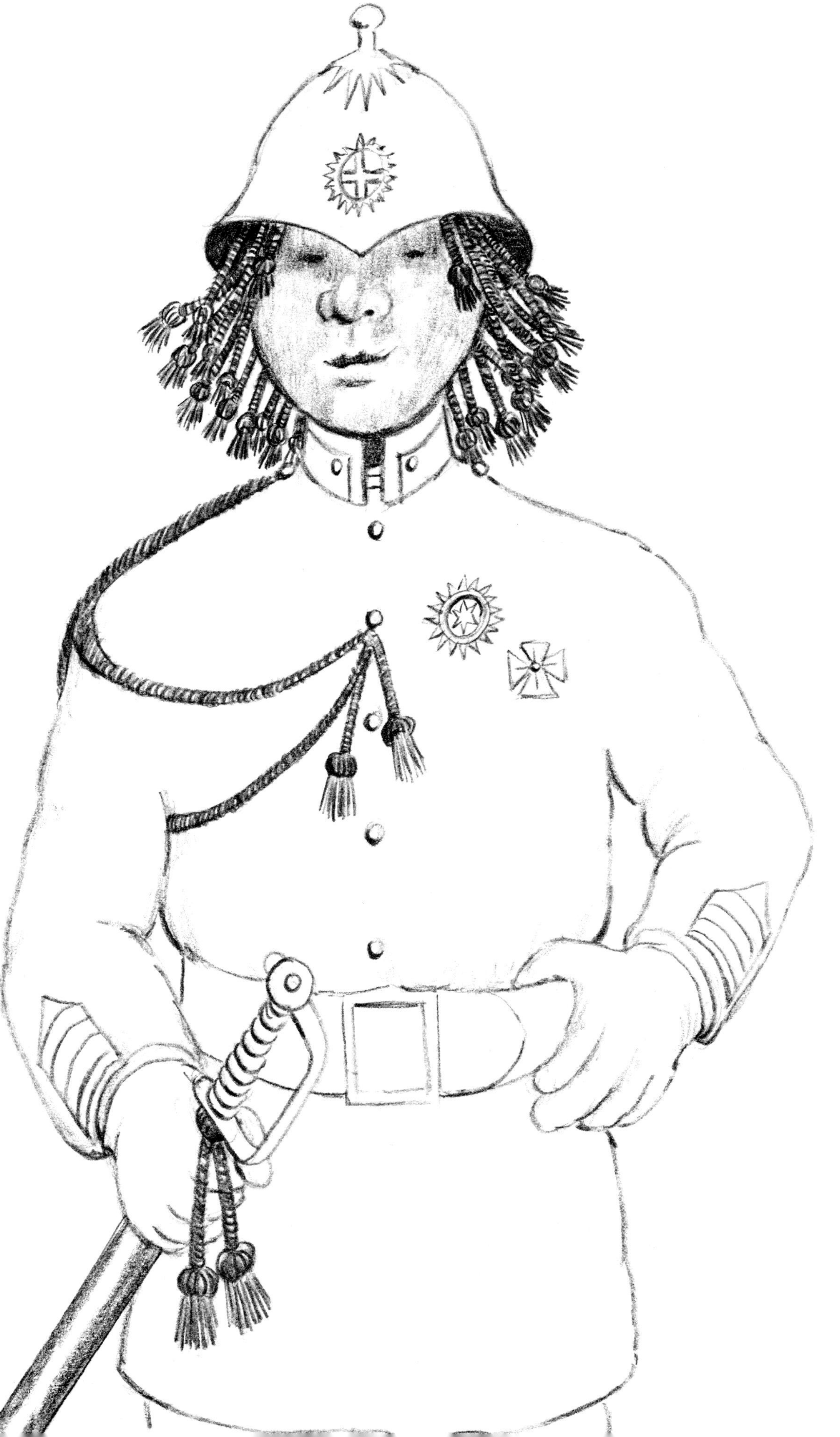

Joan Crawford Jr

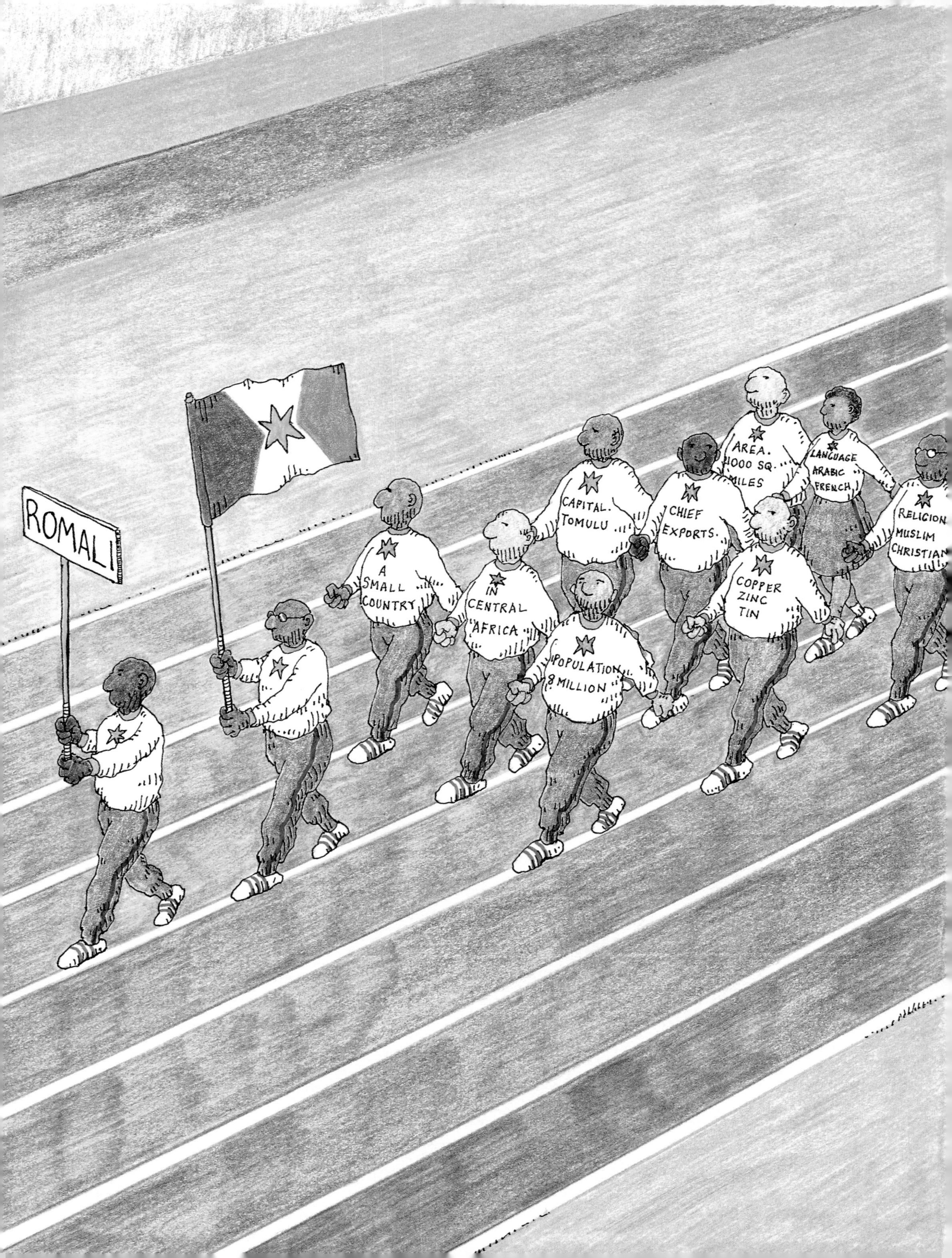
ROMALI
A SMALL COUNTRY
IN CENTRAL AFRICA
CAPITAL. TOMULU
POPULATION 8 MILLION
CHIEF EXPORTS.
COPPER ZINC TIN
AREA. 1000 SQ. MILES
LANGUAGE ARABIC FRENCH
RELIGION MUSLIM CHRISTIAN

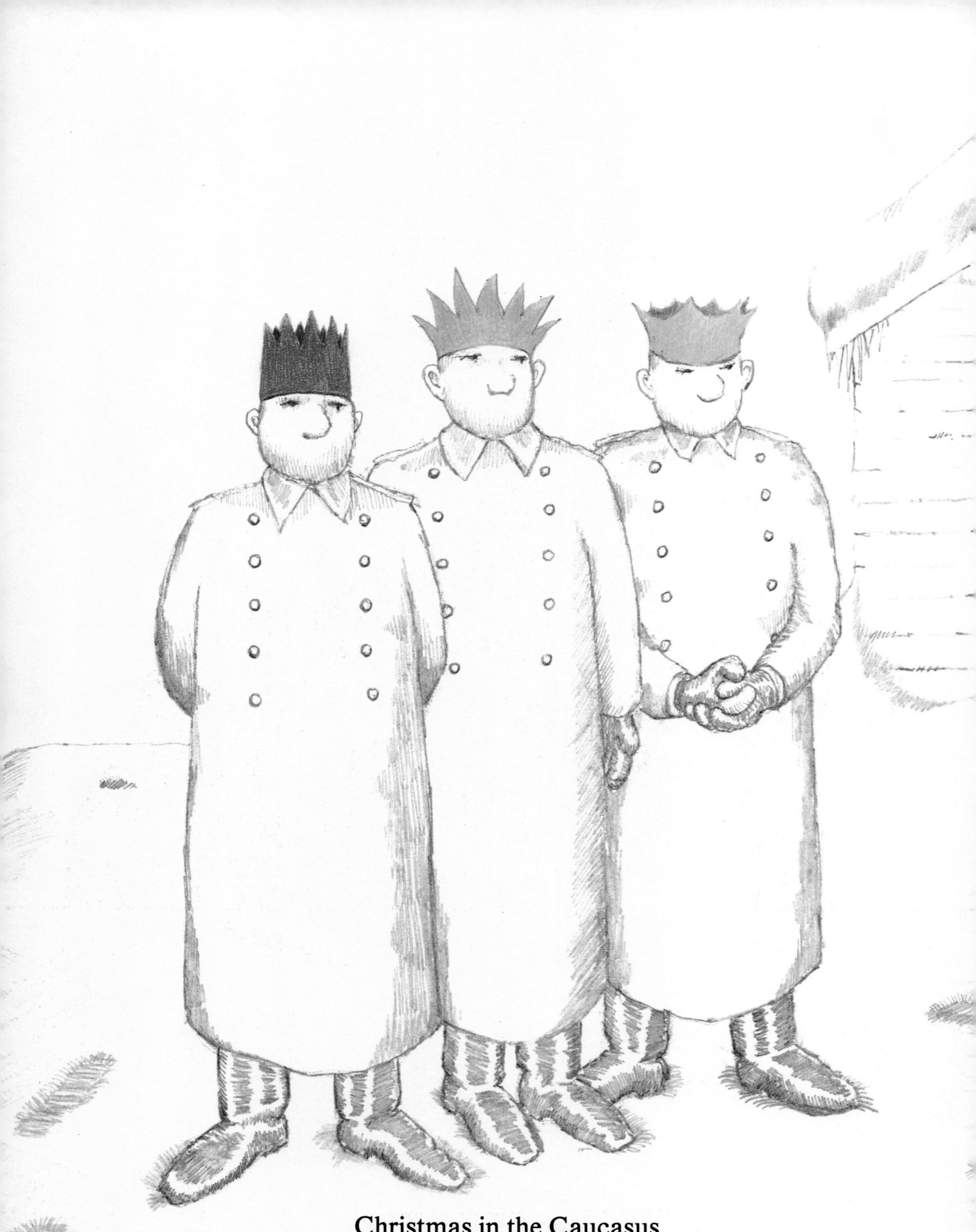

Christmas in the Caucasus

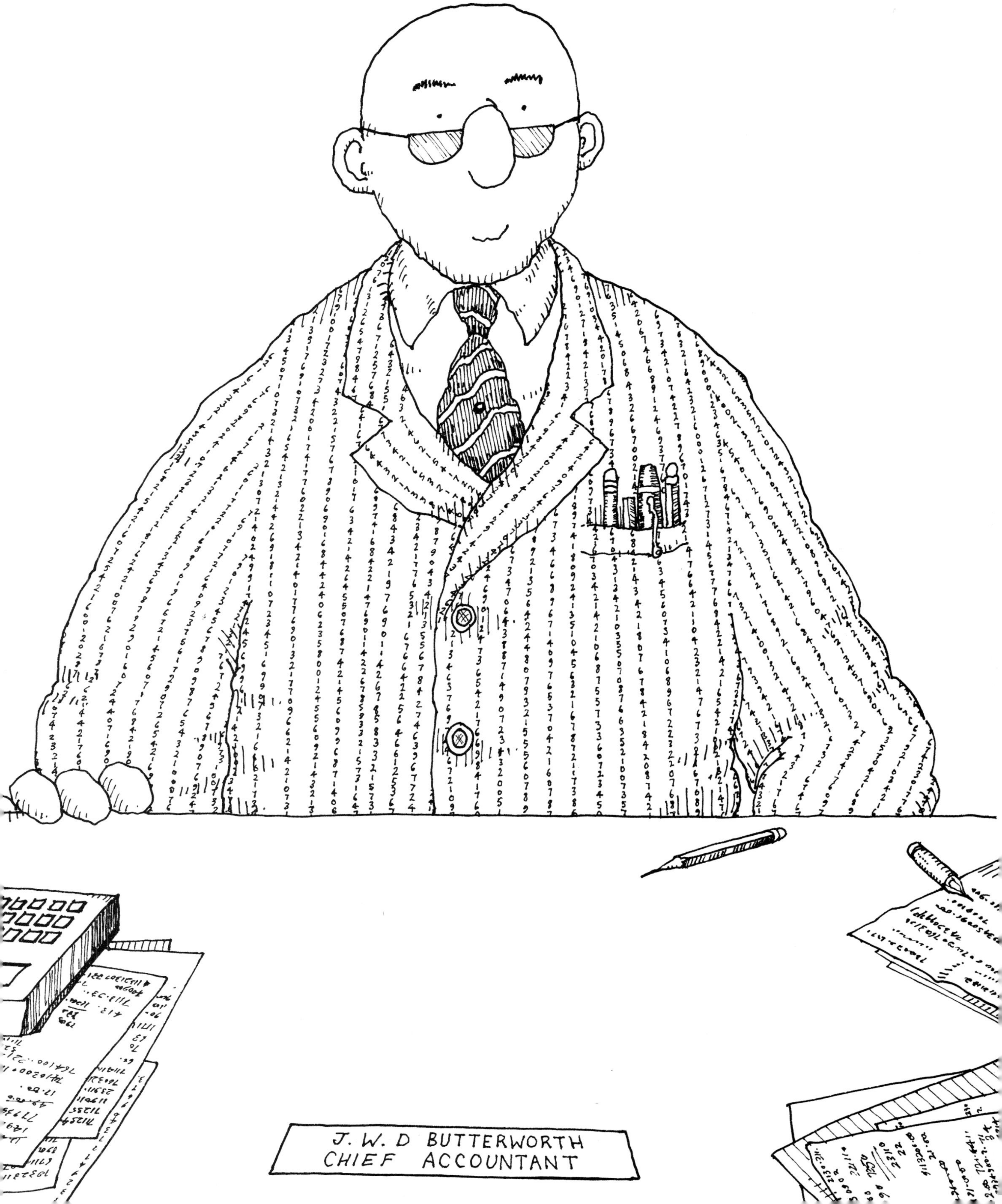
J. W. D BUTTERWORTH
CHIEF ACCOUNTANT

The Purist's Pinstripe

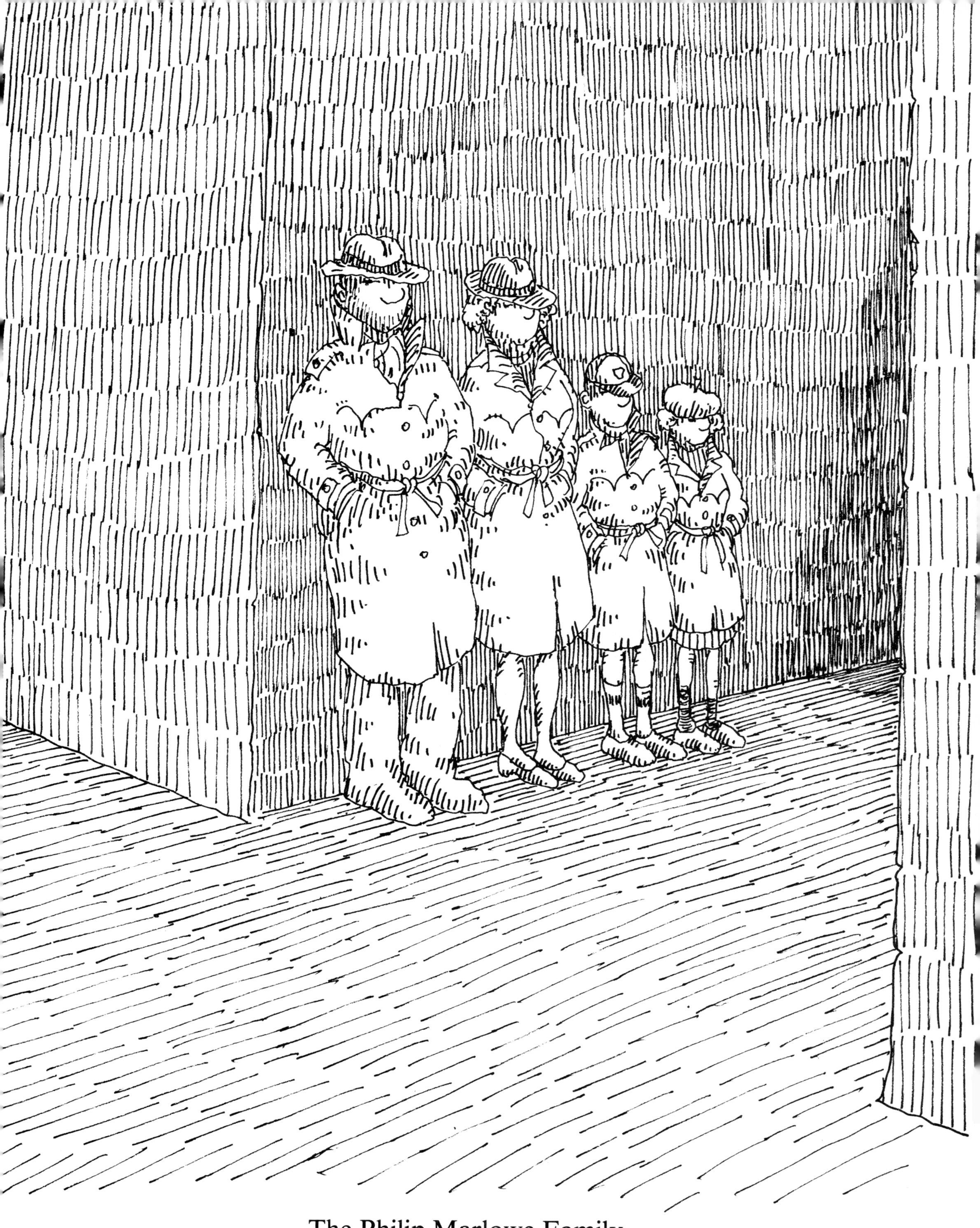

The Philip Marlowe Family

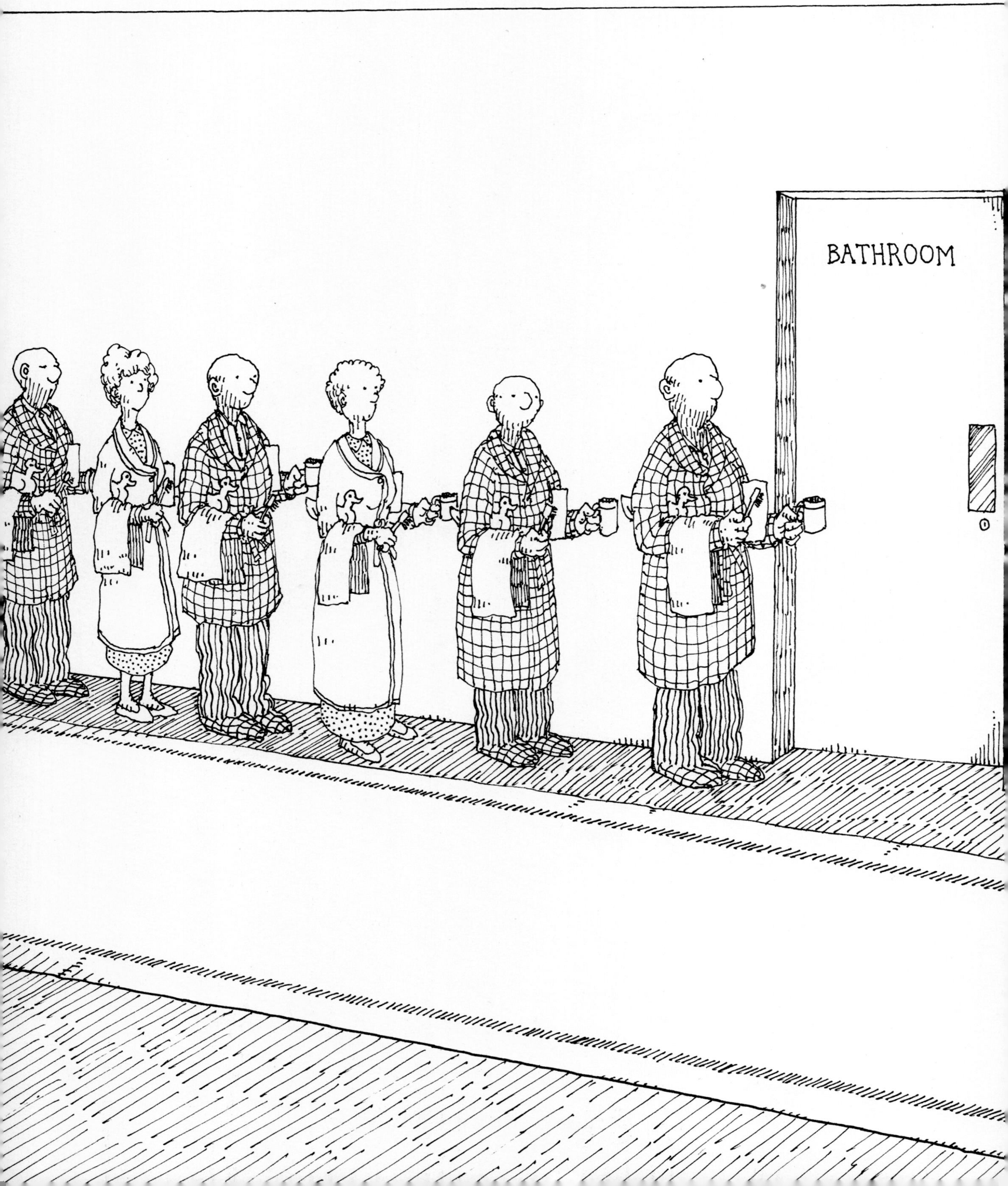
BATHROOM

Savile Row
Surprise

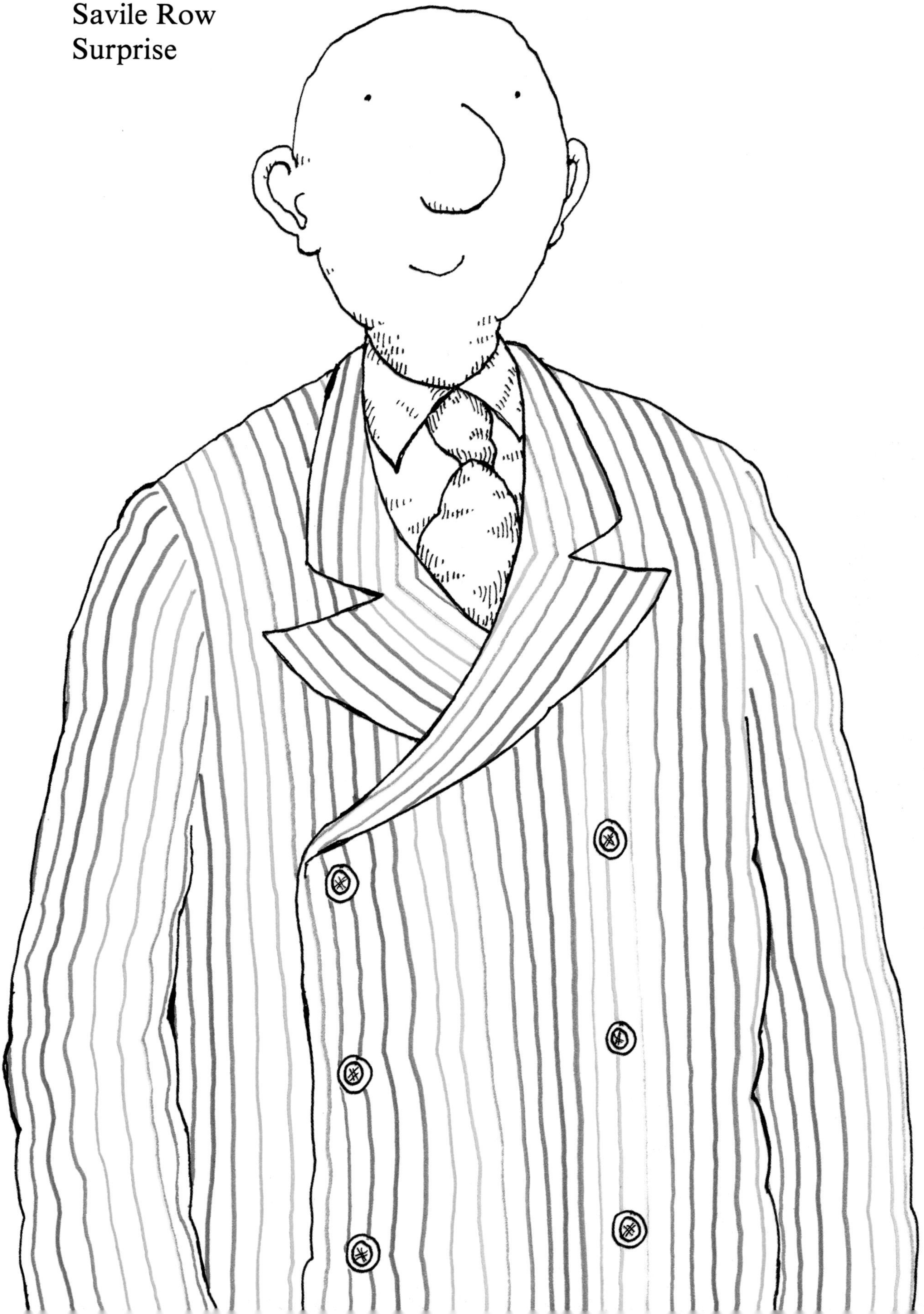

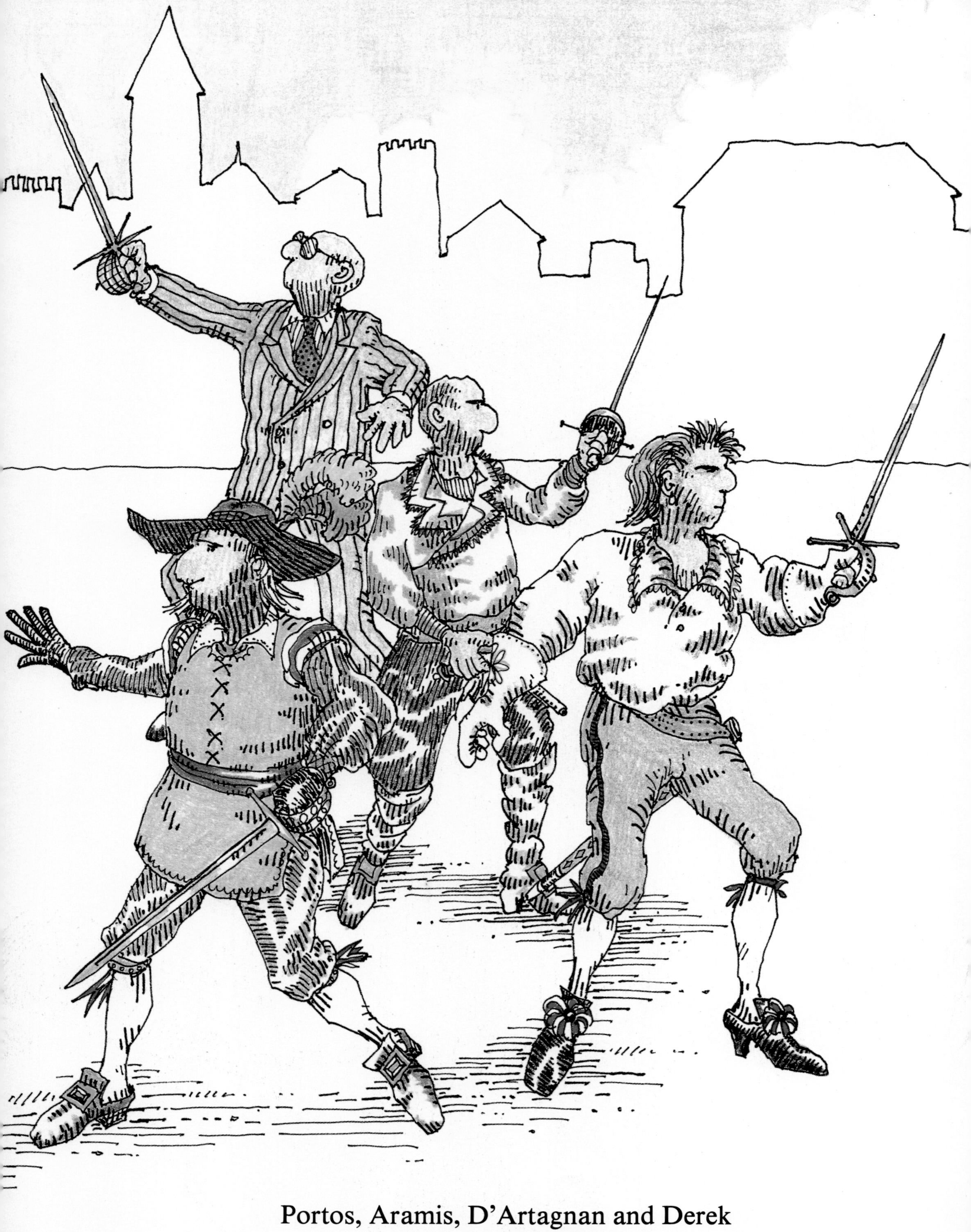

Portos, Aramis, D'Artagnan and Derek

B.T.S.A.K.A.
(Before the Swiss
Army Knife Arrived)

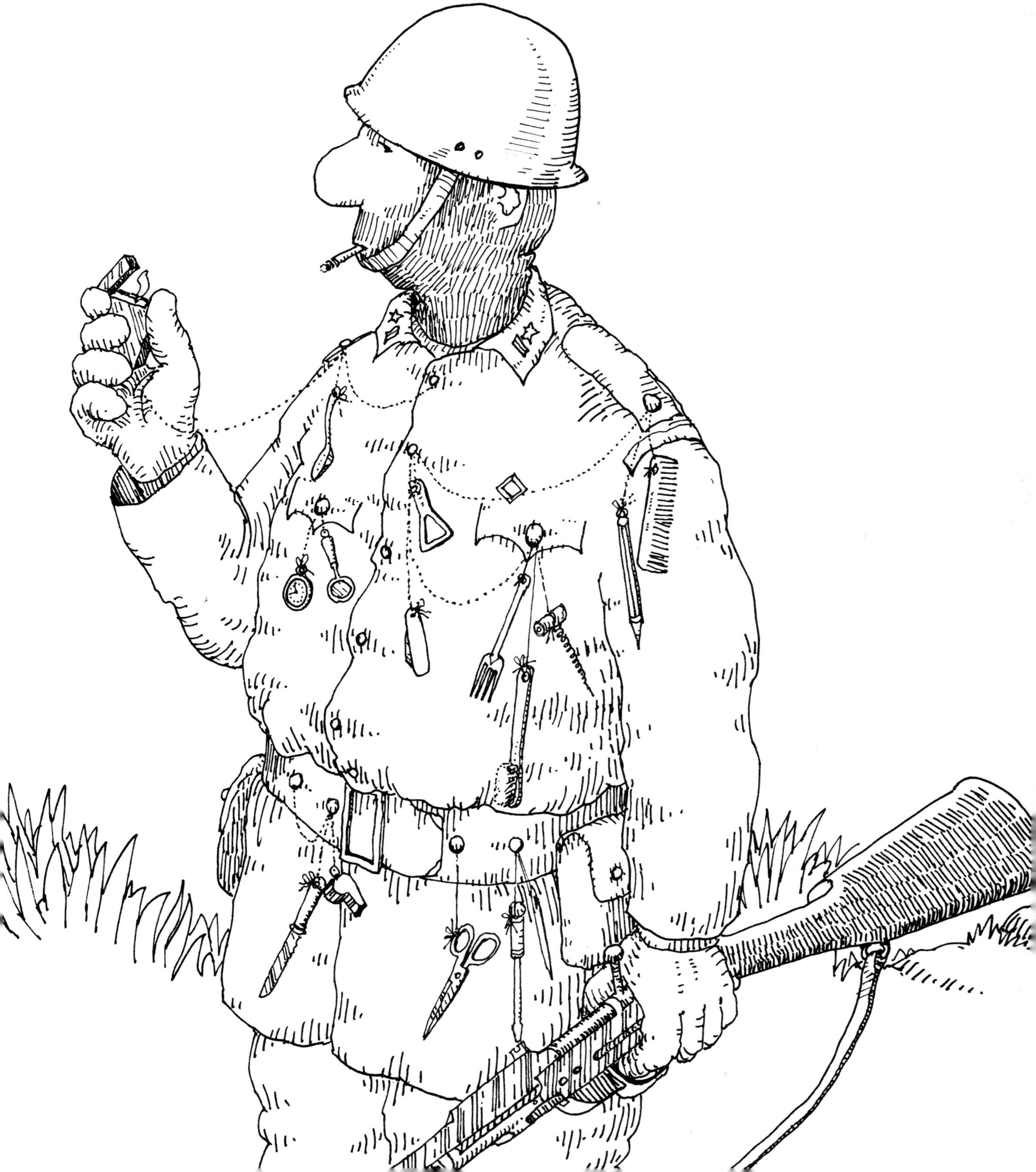

Following in Father's Footsteps

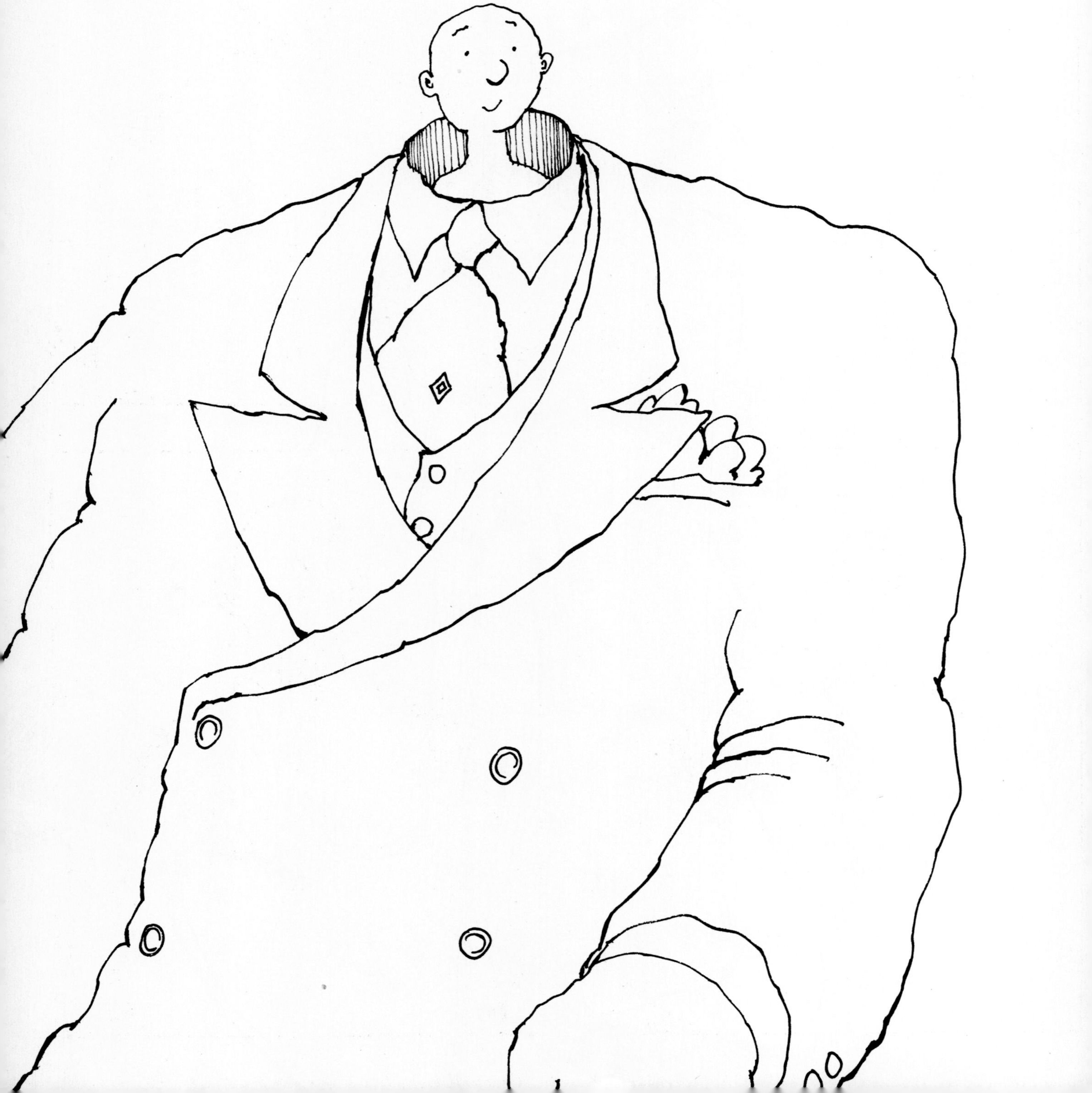

THE FOUR SEASONS

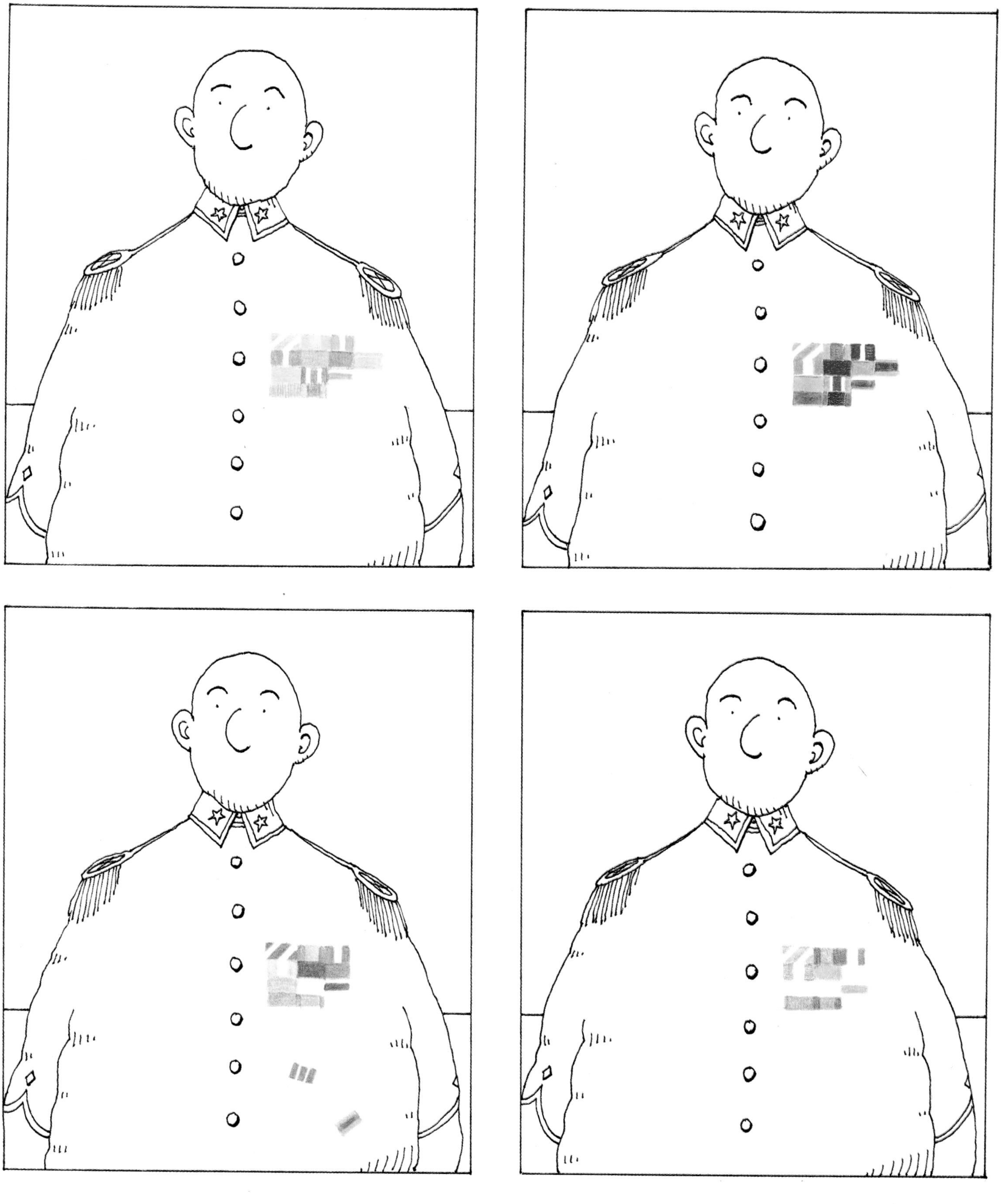

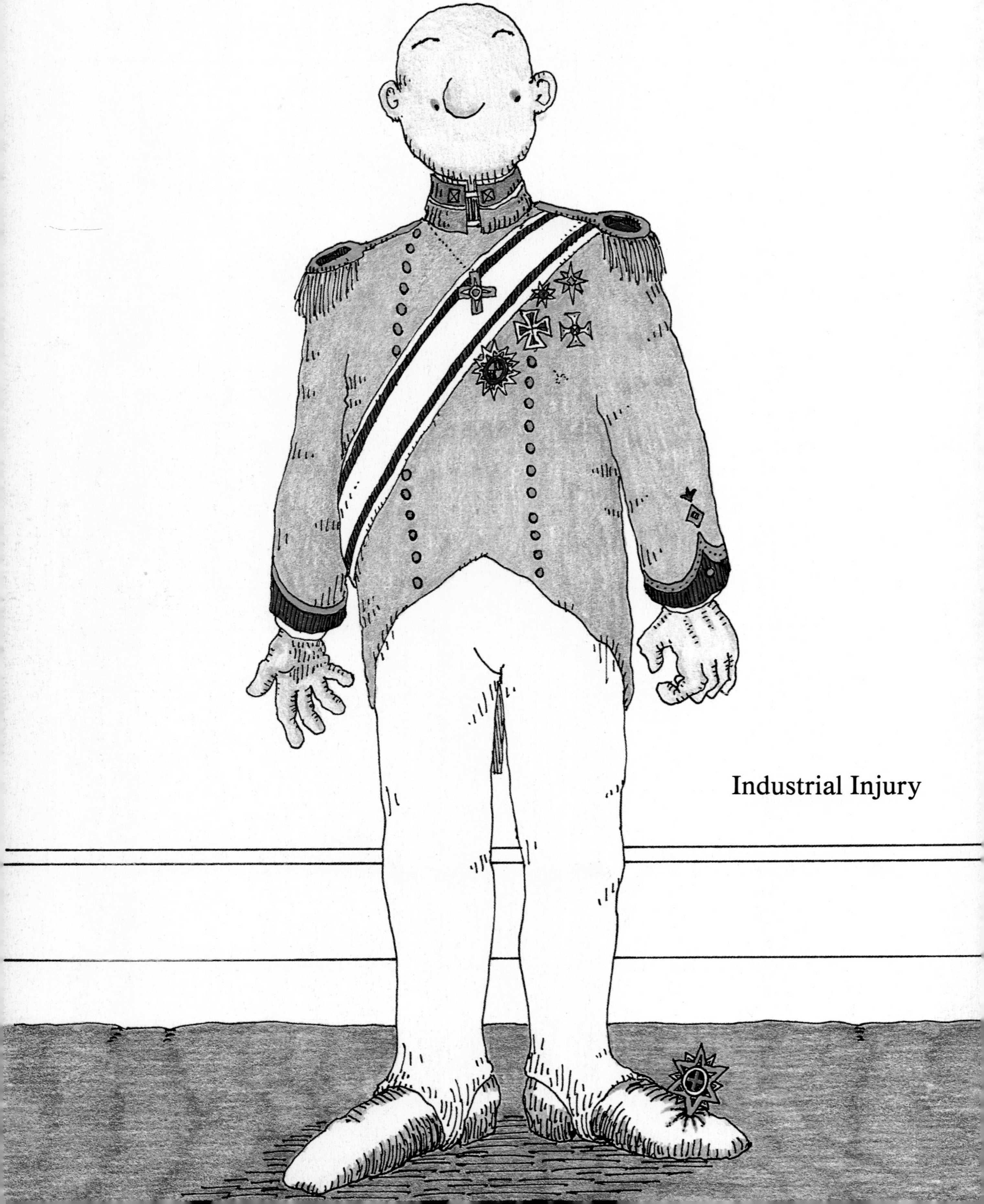

Industrial Injury

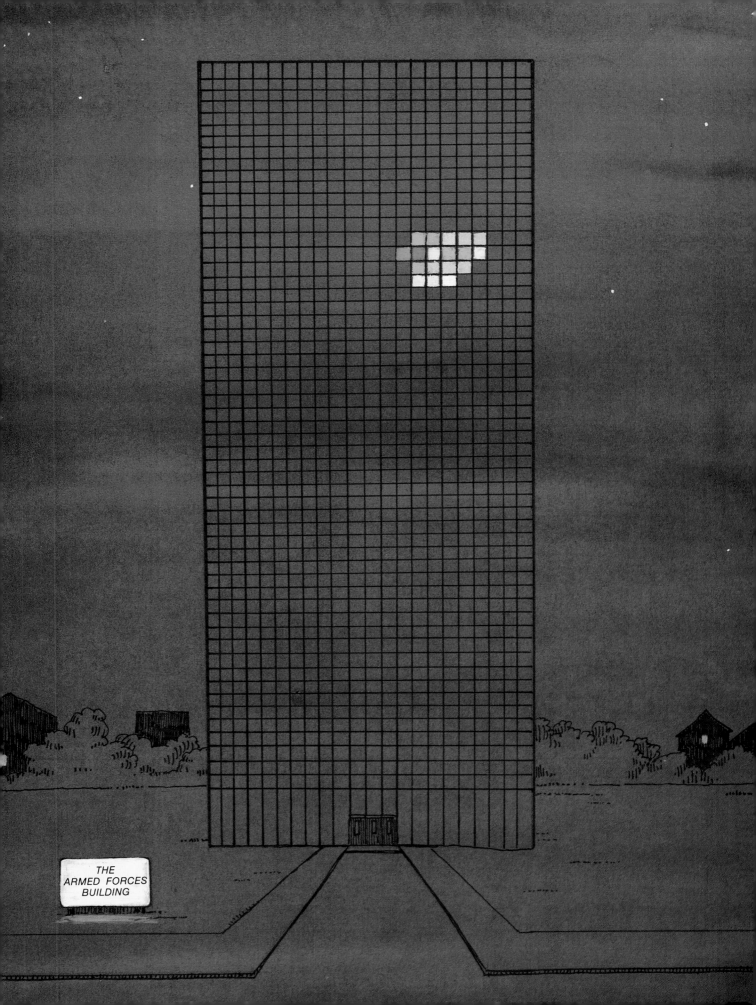

THE
ARMED FORCES
BUILDING

'How about a game of strip poker?'

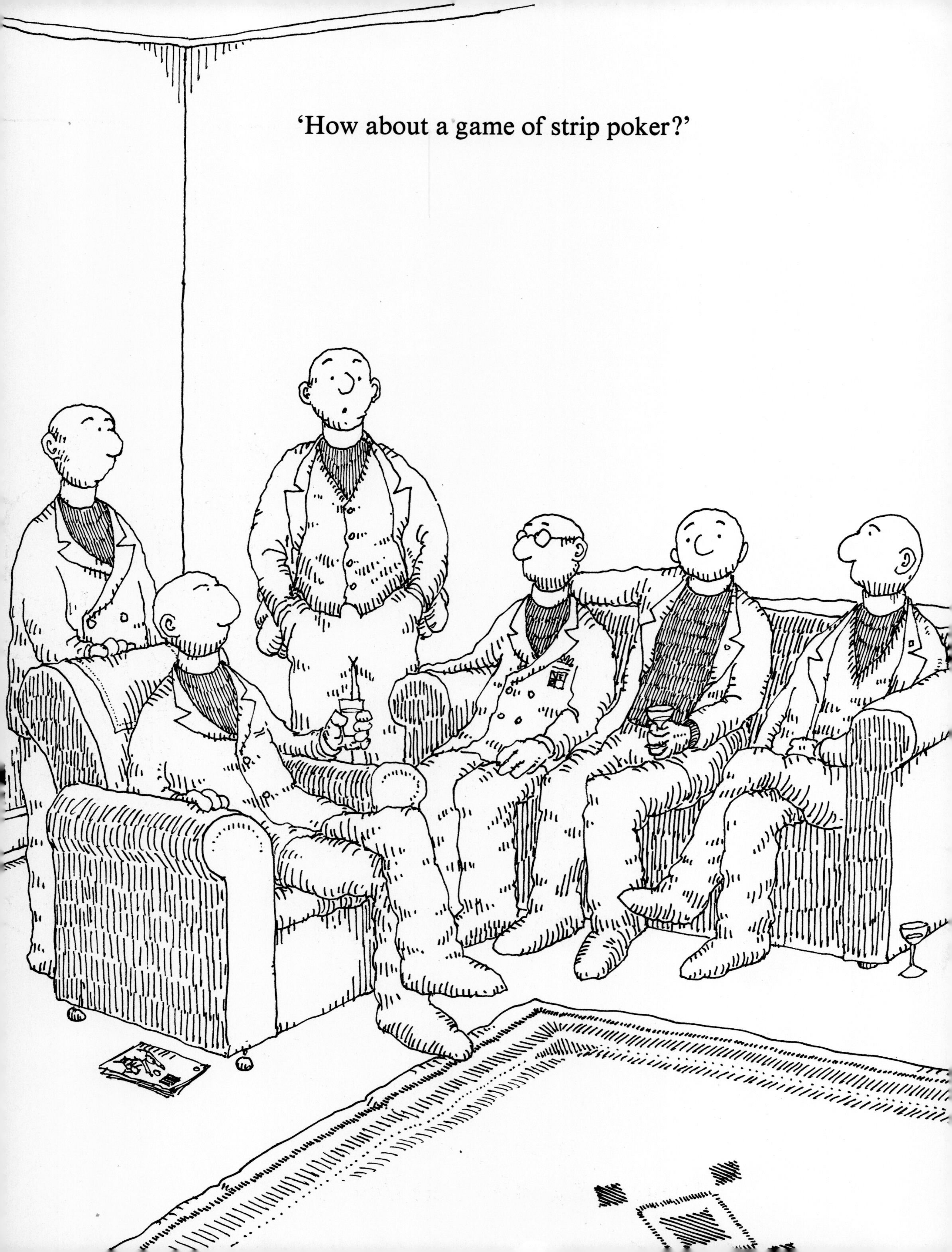

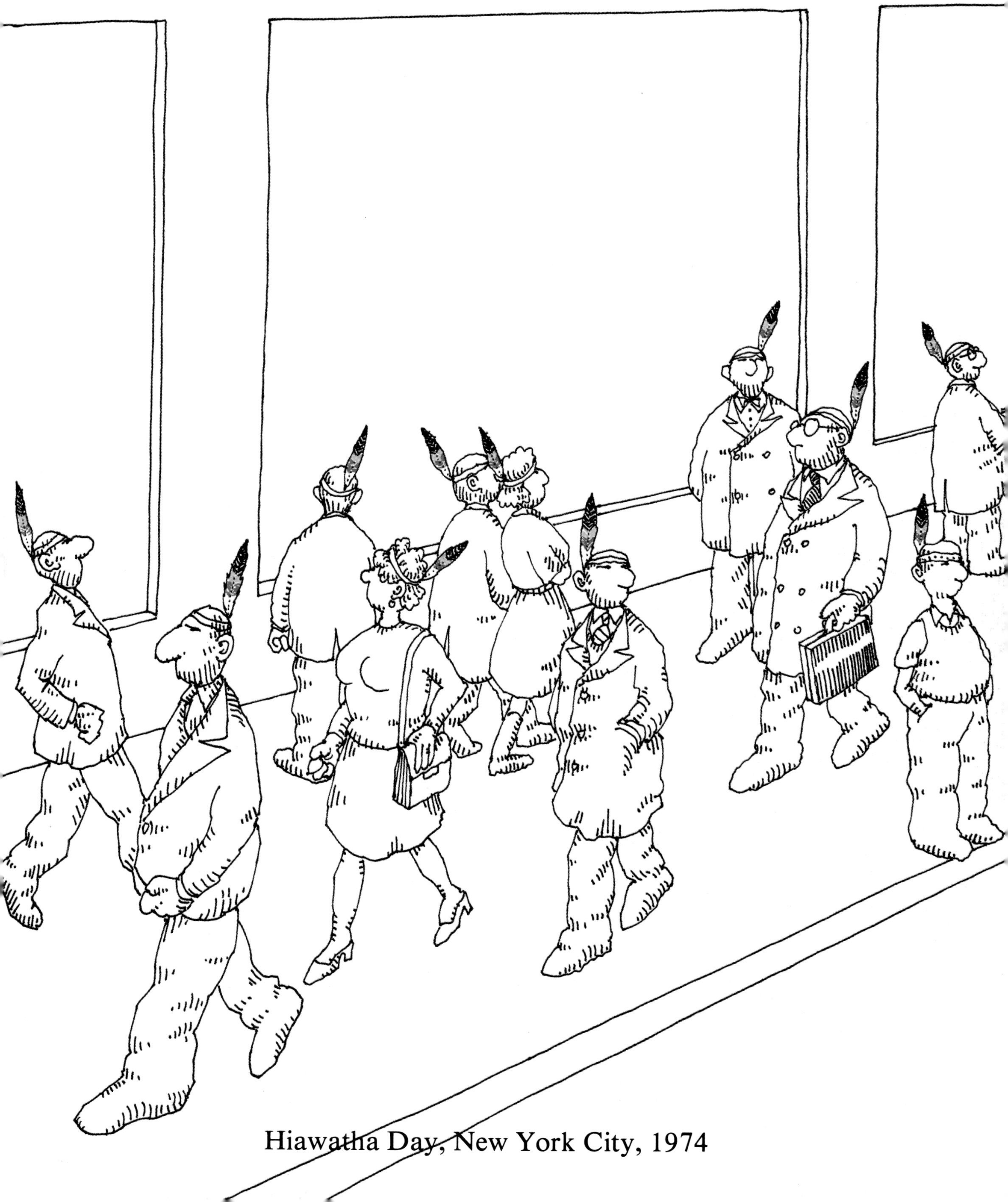

Hiawatha Day, New York City, 1974

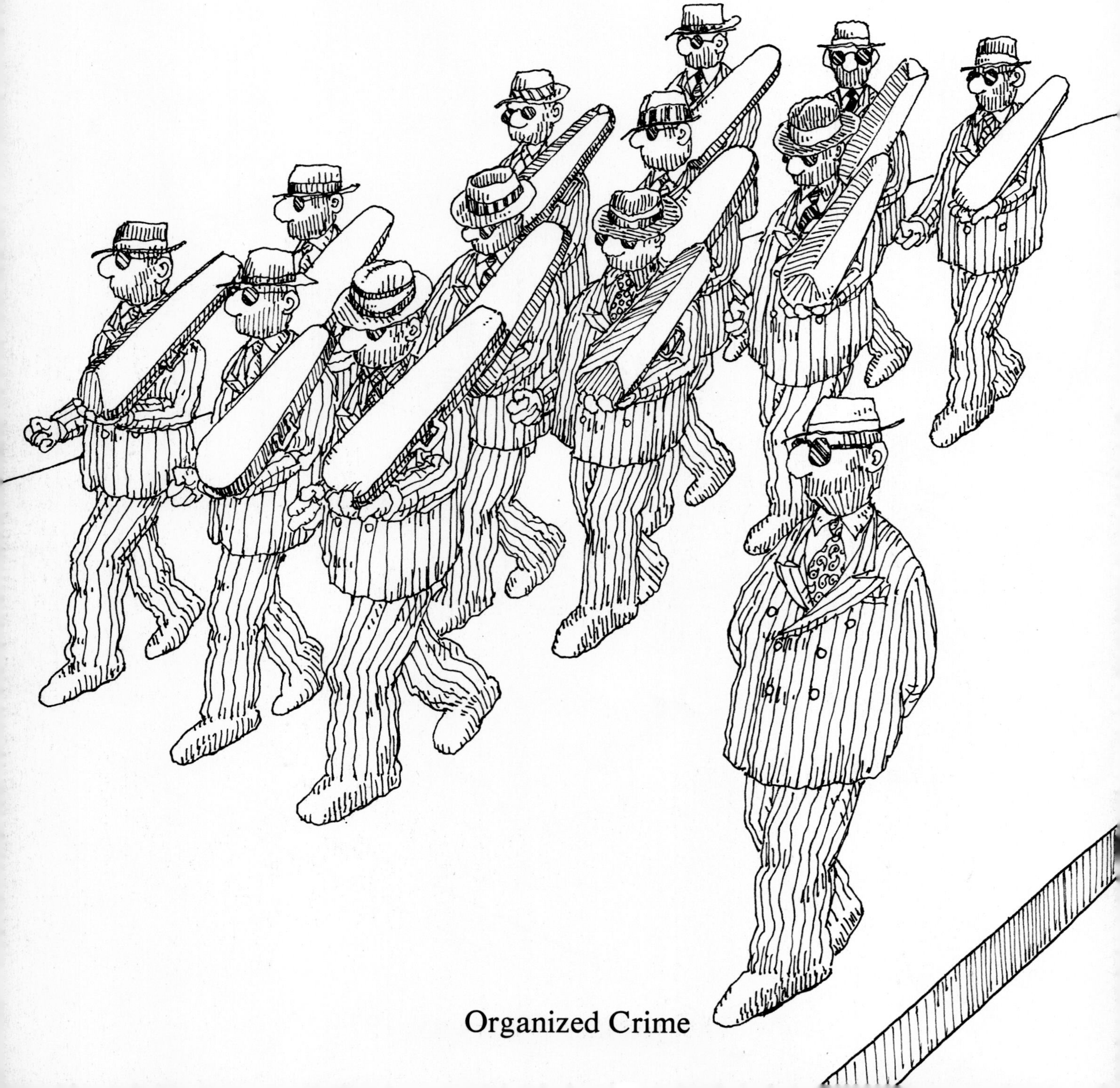

Organized Crime

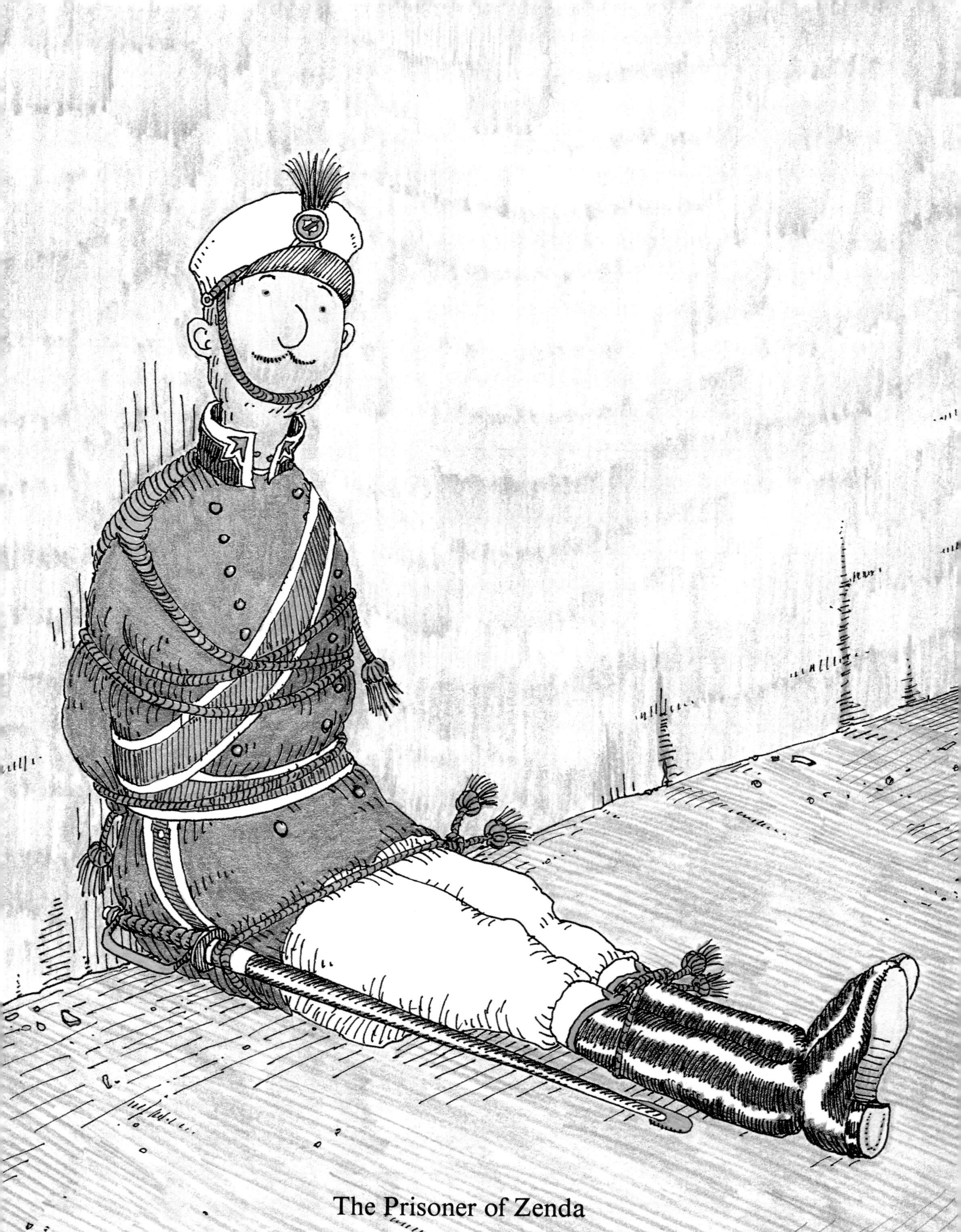

The Prisoner of Zenda

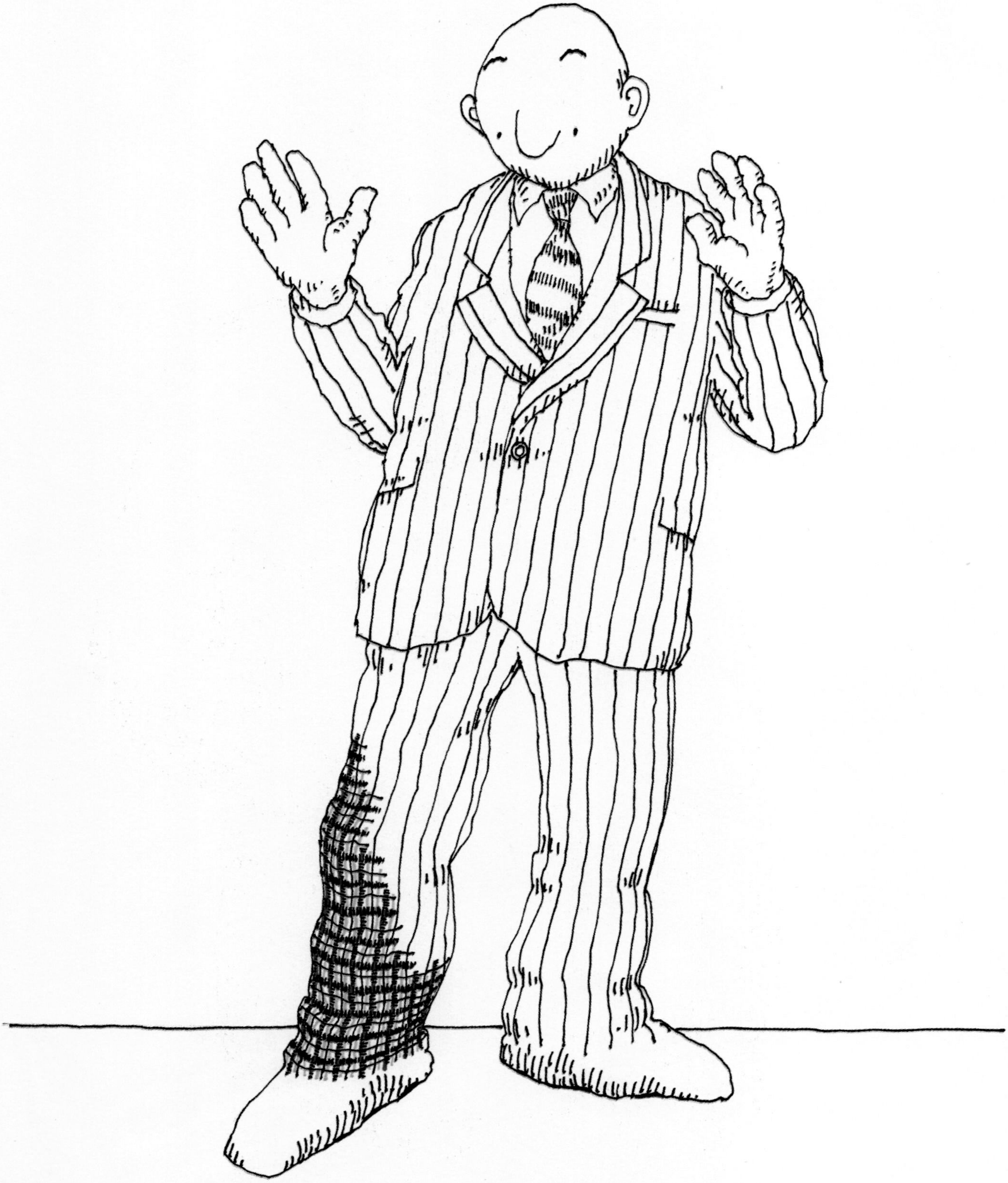

A Sudden Attack of the Plaid

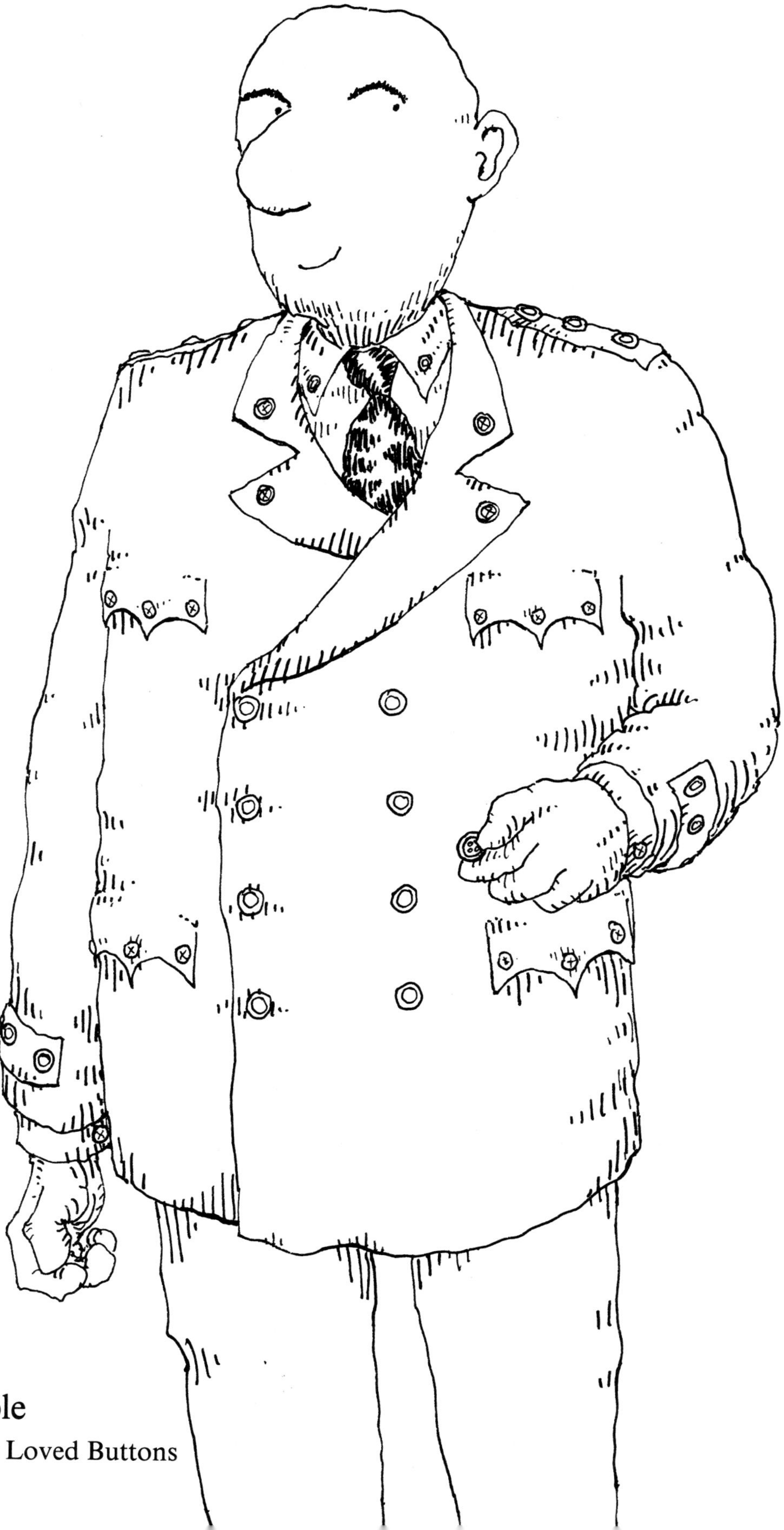

Digby Ripple
The Man Who Loved Buttons

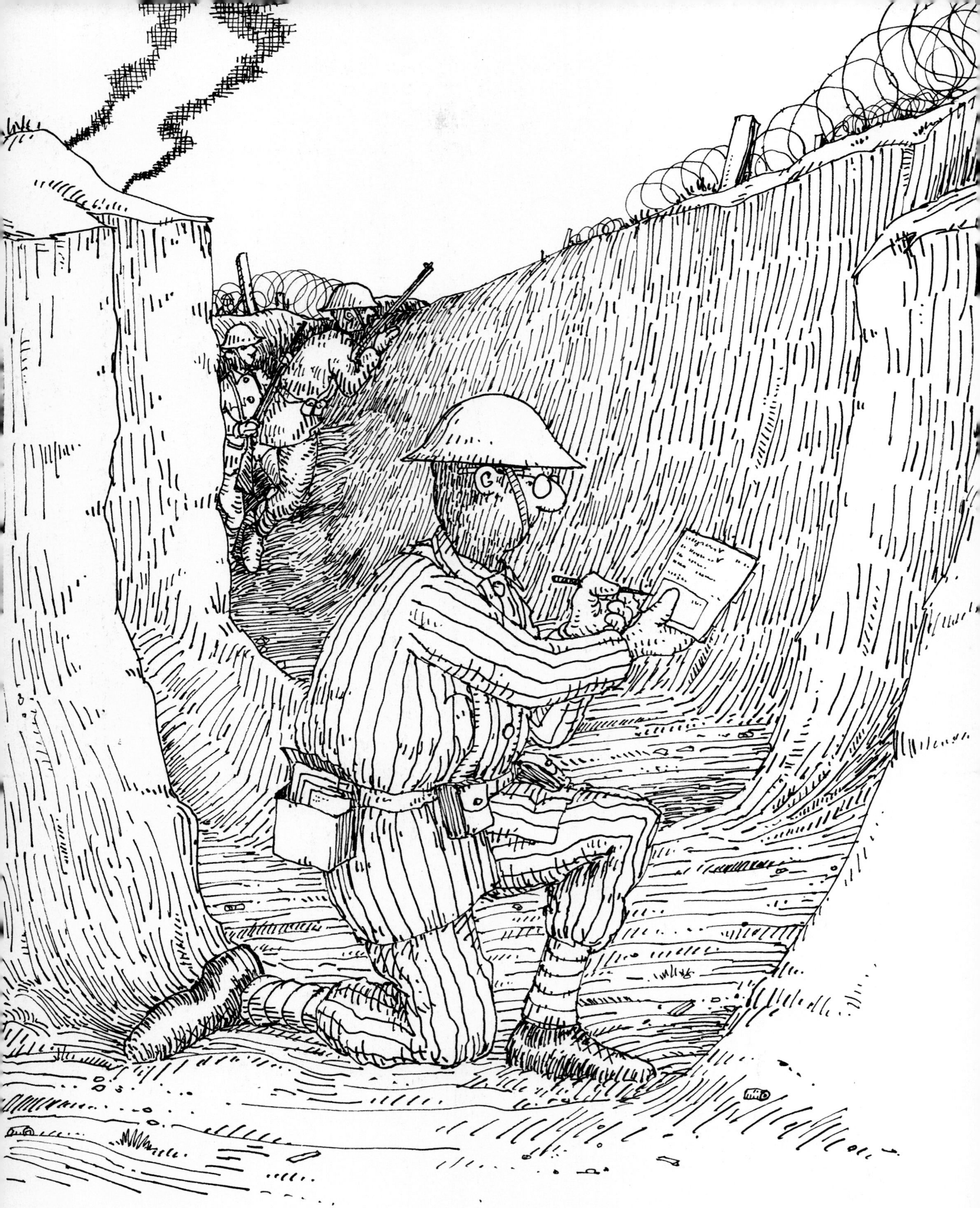

Royal London Yeomanry (Clerical Officer)

THE COMEDIANS

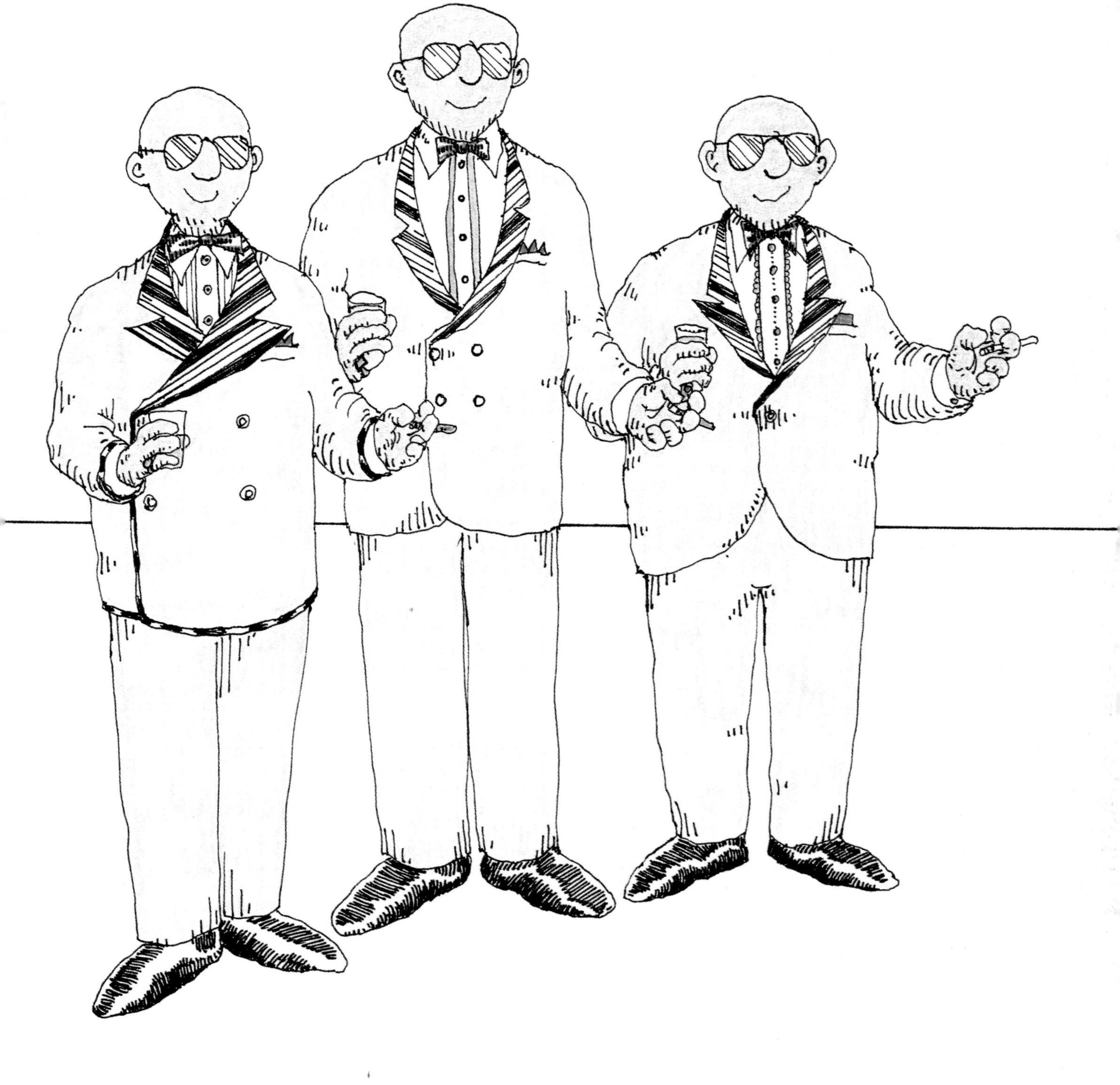

The Dress Uniform of a Private,
Catering Corps

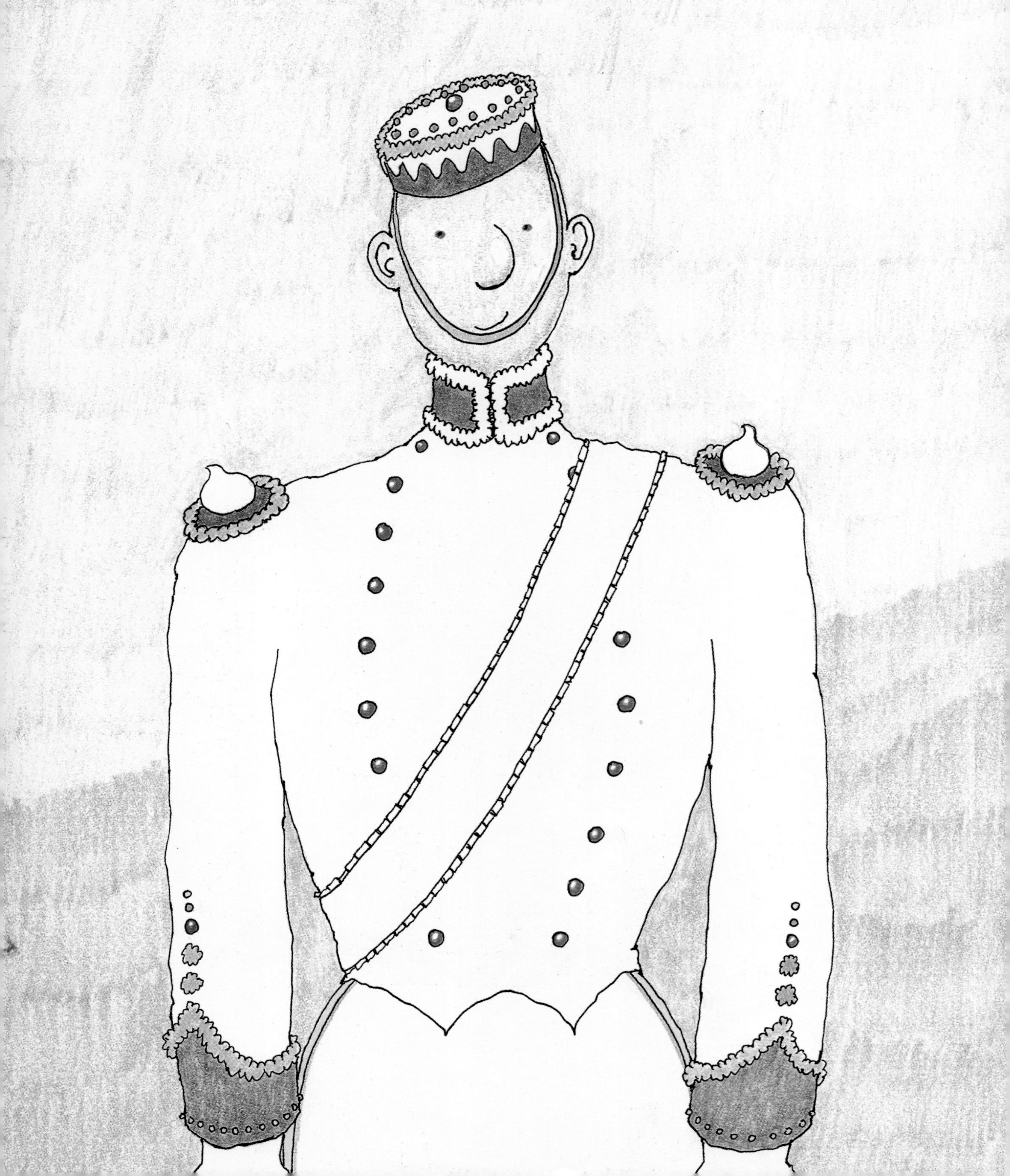

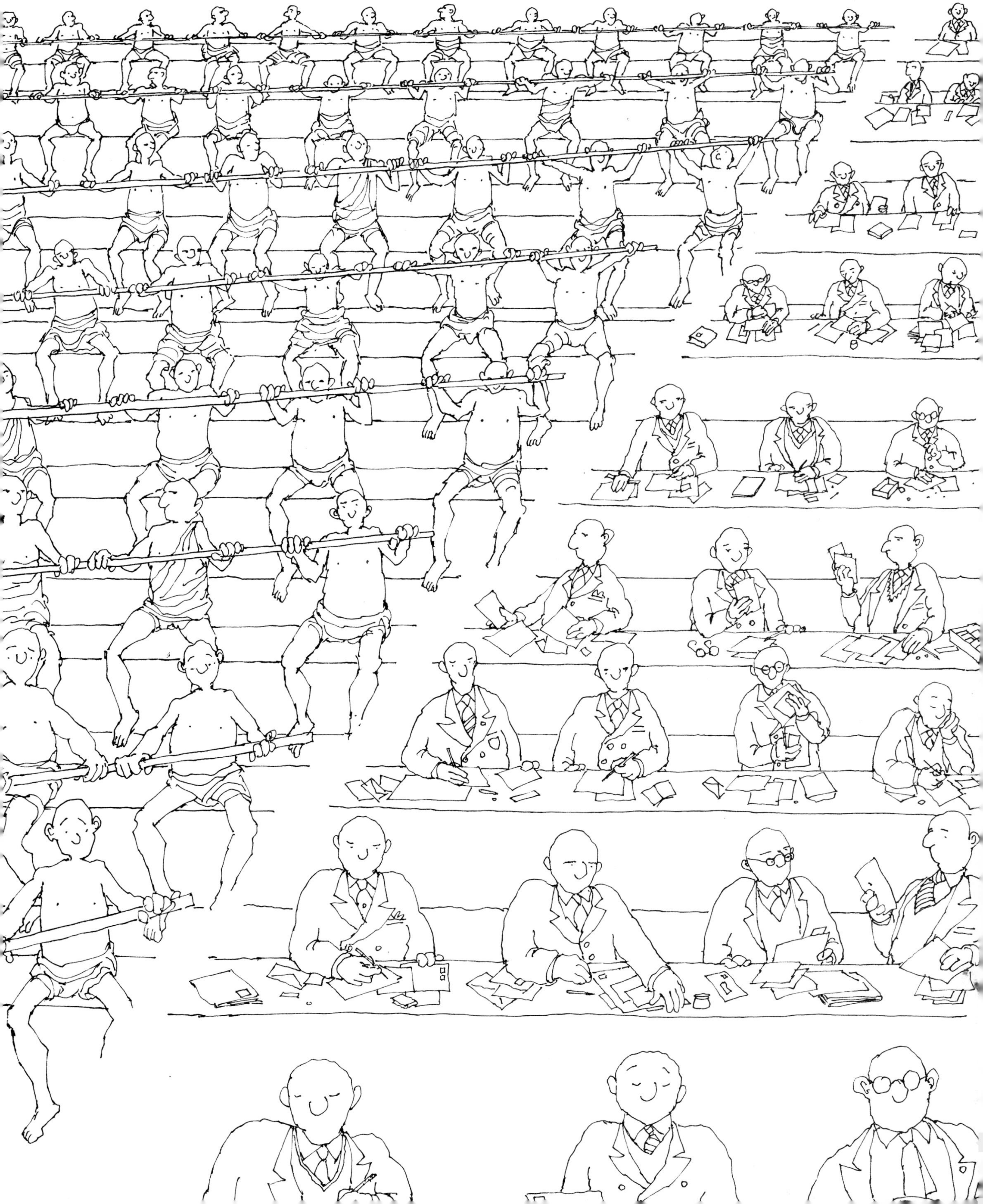

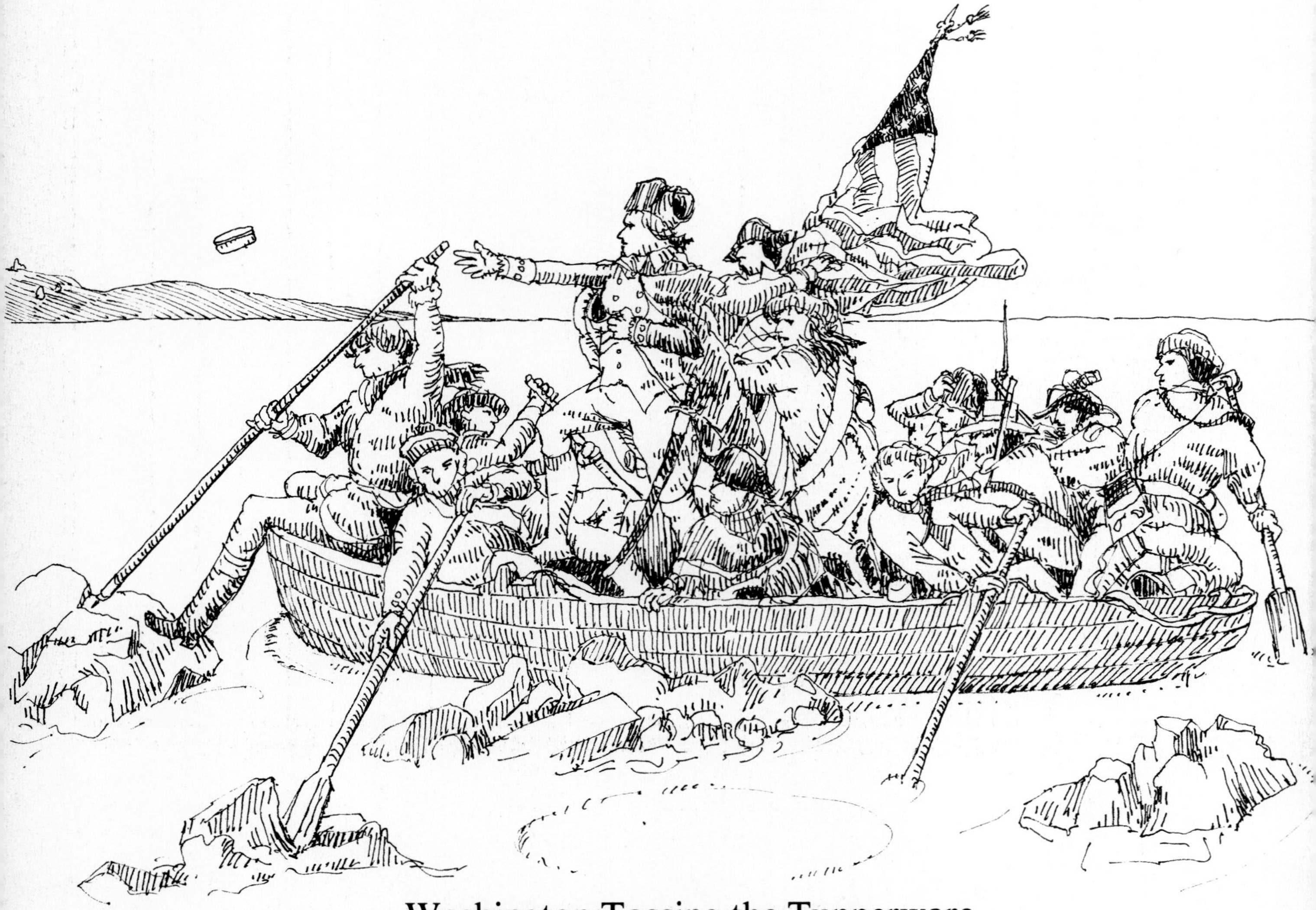

Washington Tossing the Tupperware

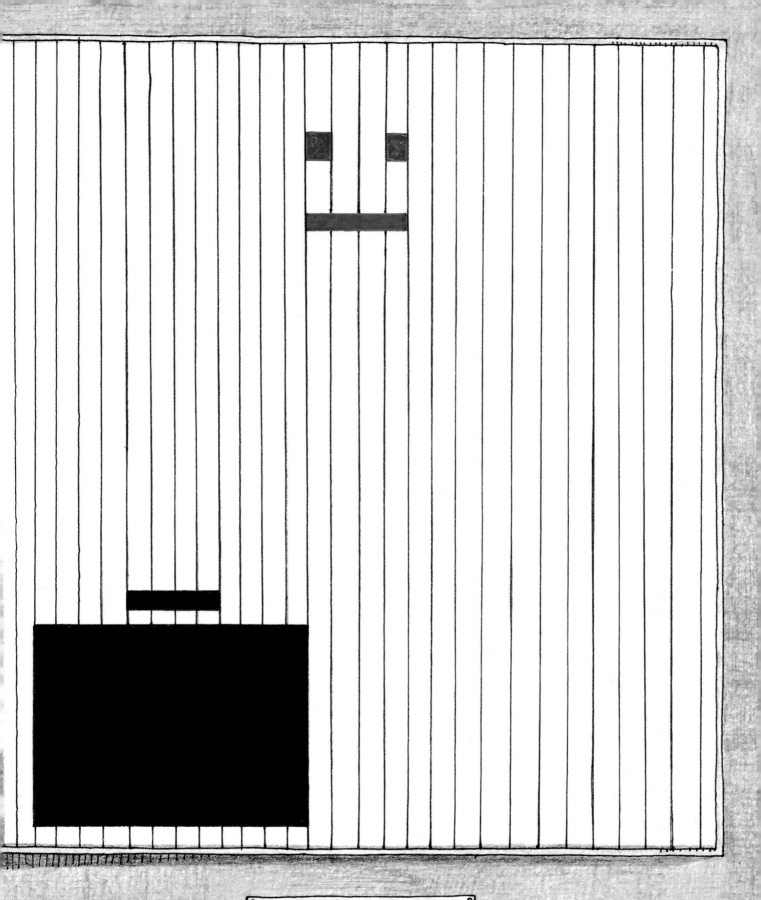

PIET MONDRIAN 1927
THE ACCOUNTANT

Nepotism

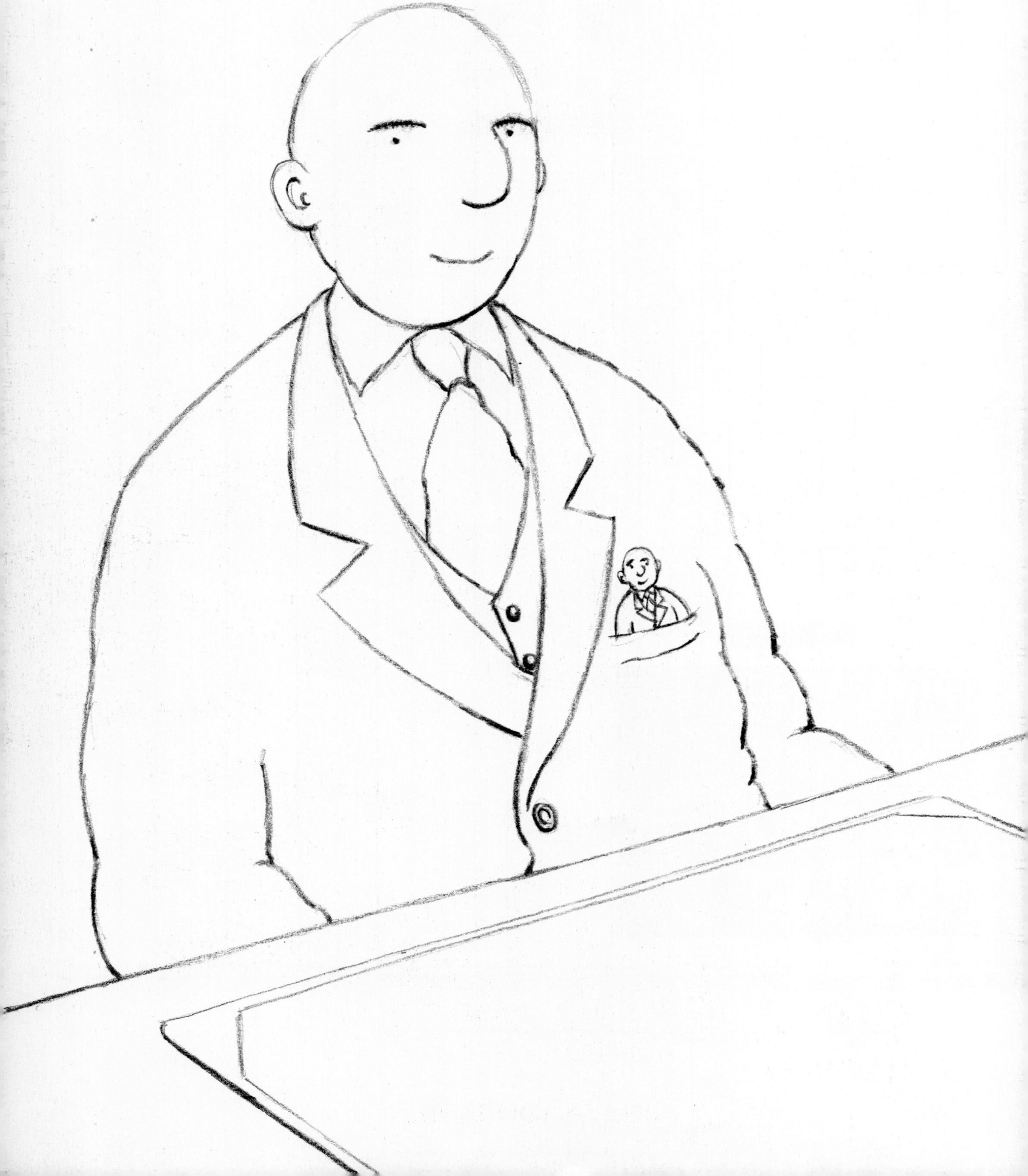

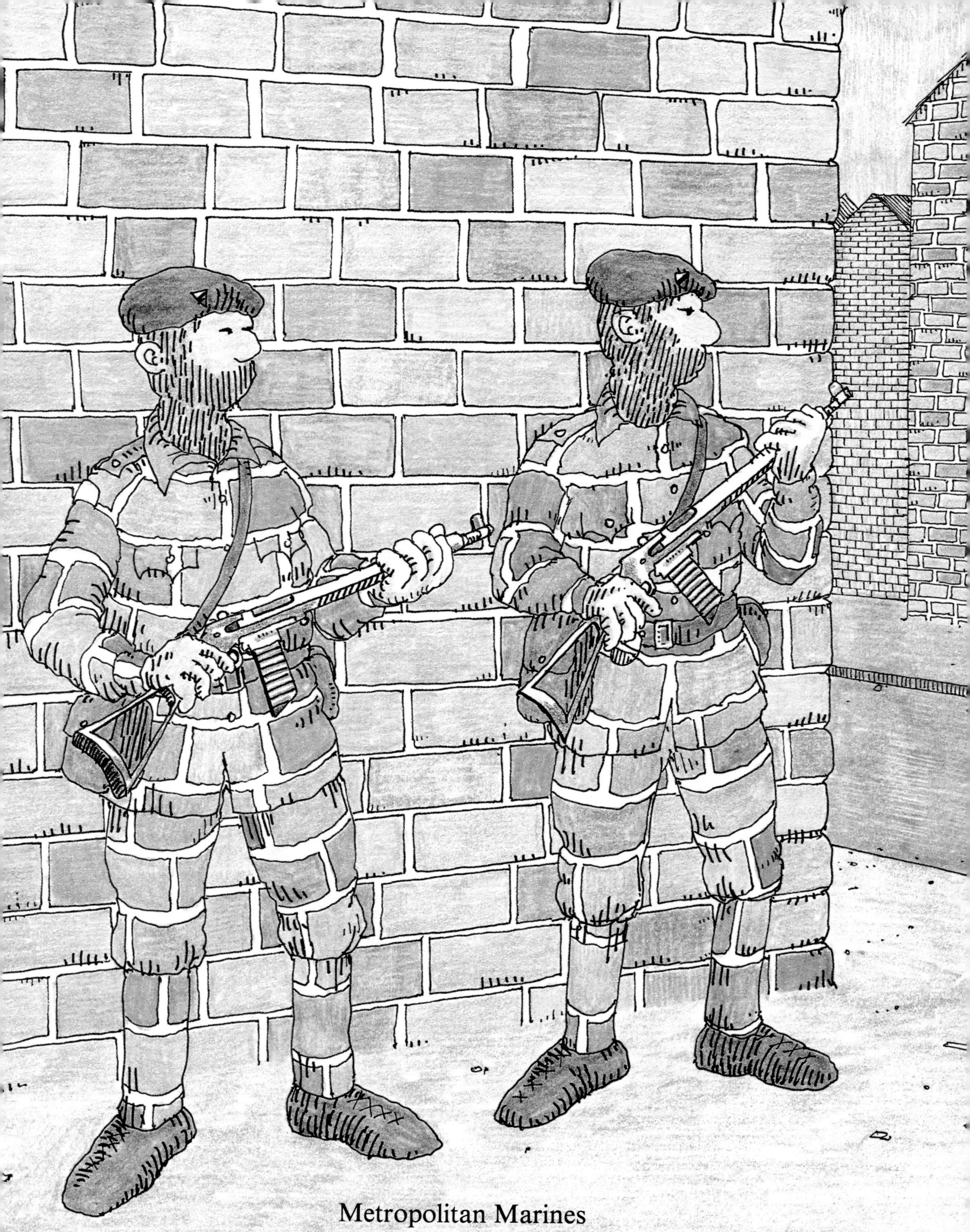

Metropolitan Marines

Samuel Finley Breese Morse
1791-1872

Inventor of Morse Code

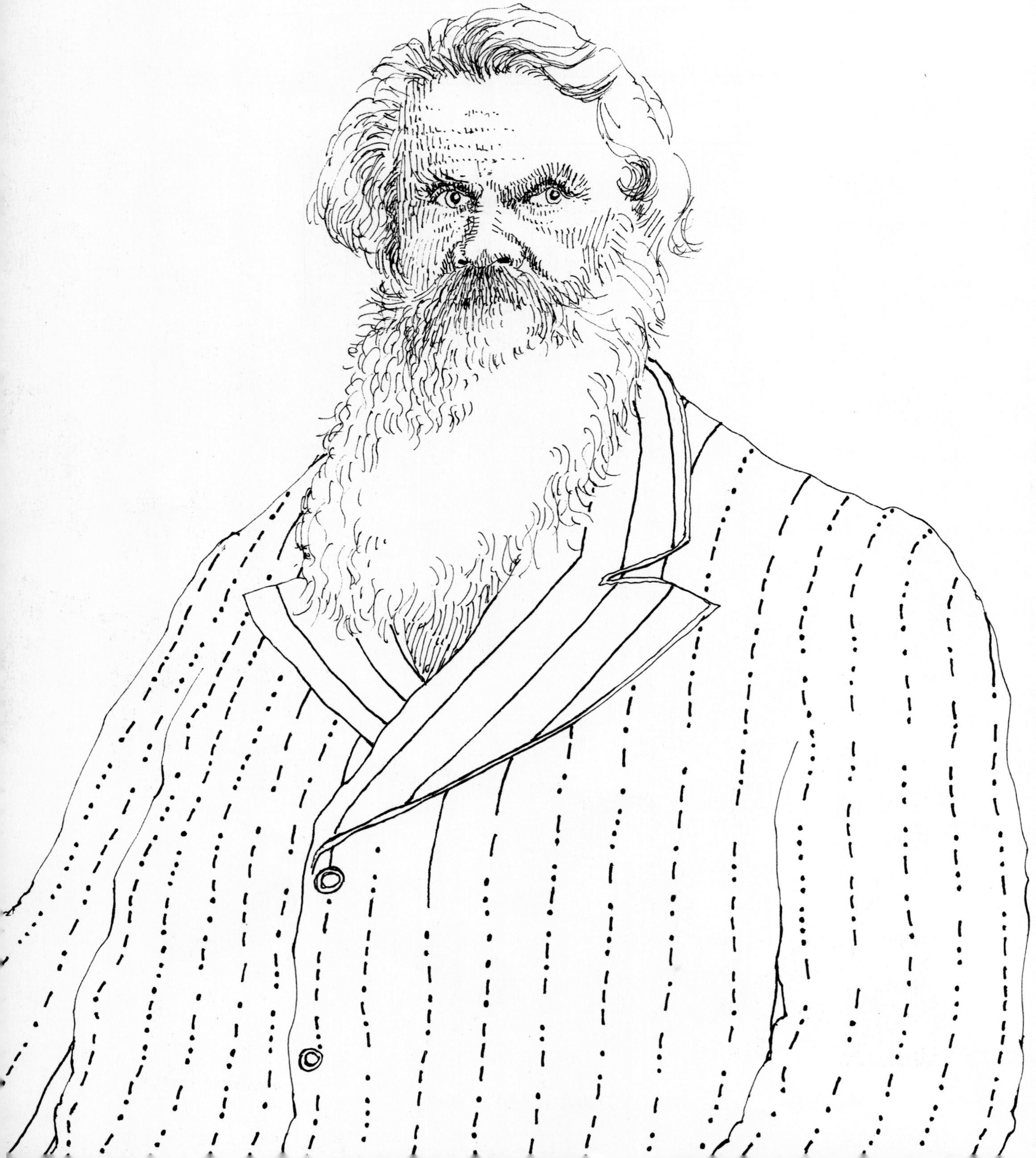

Washday in a Small Republic

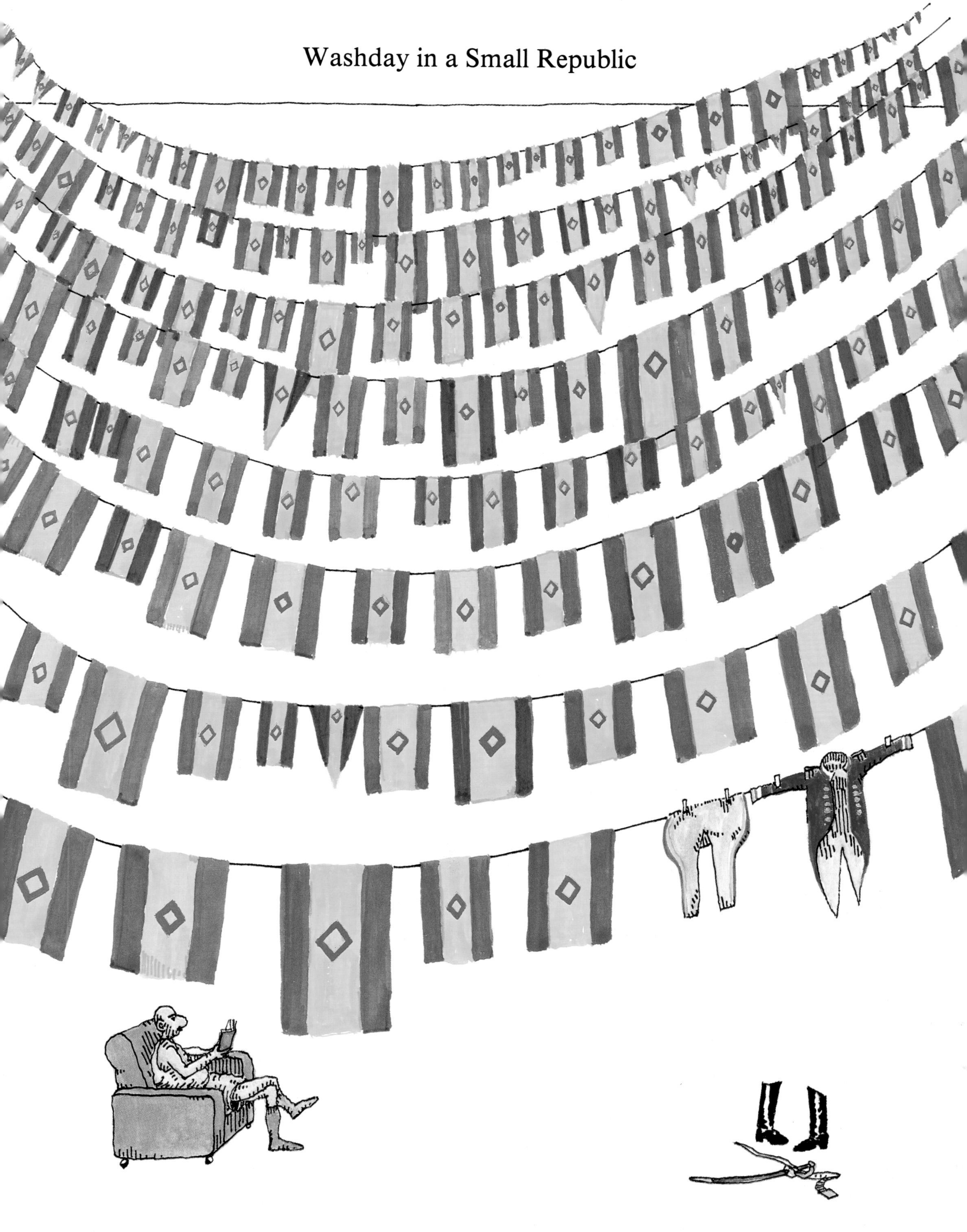

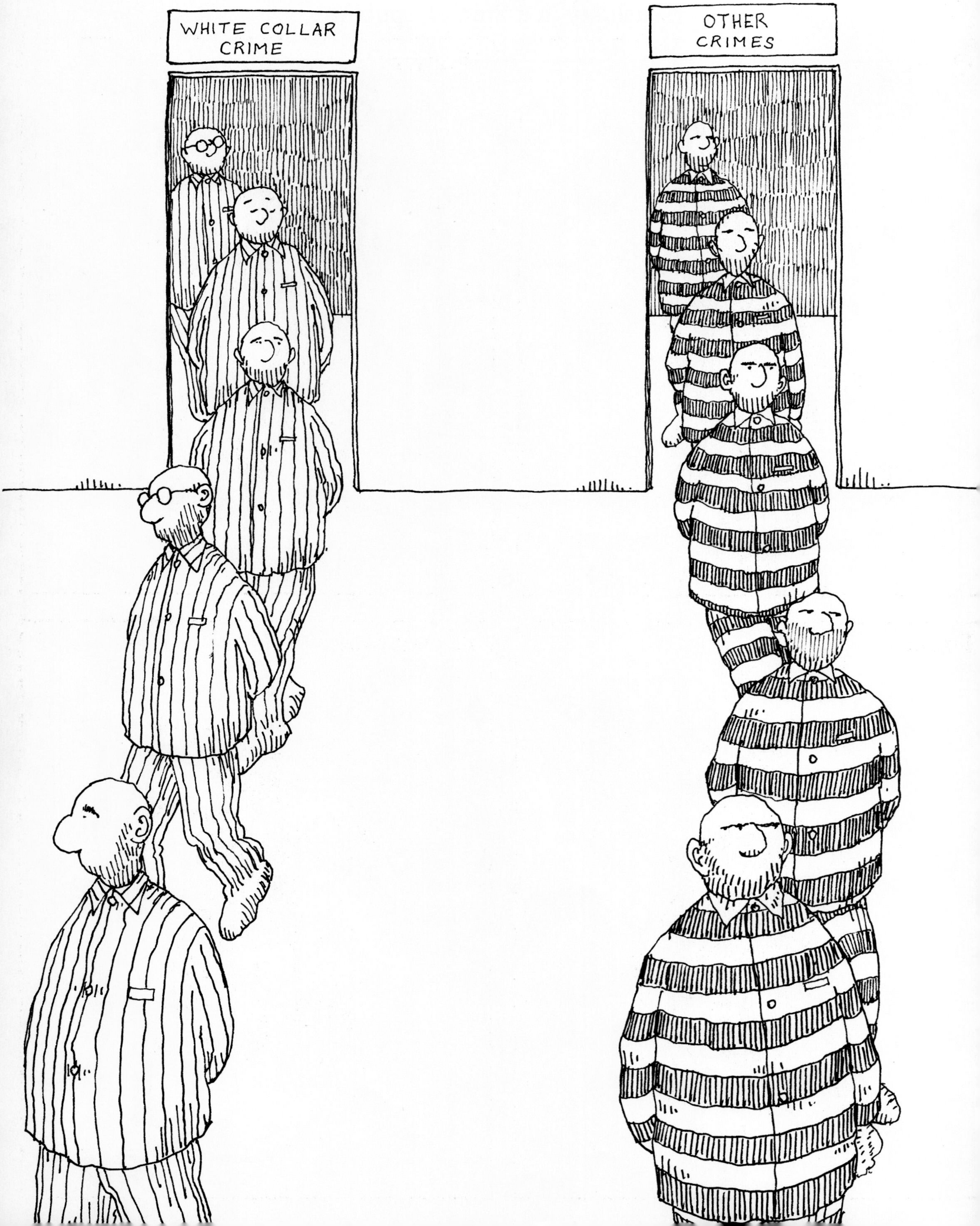
WHITE COLLAR CRIME
OTHER CRIMES

Queen

Worker

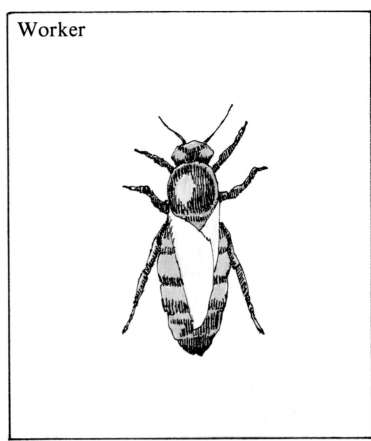

Drone

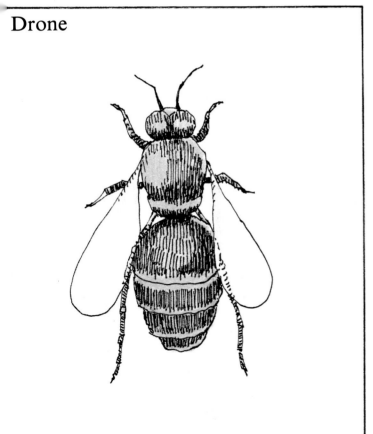

Accountant

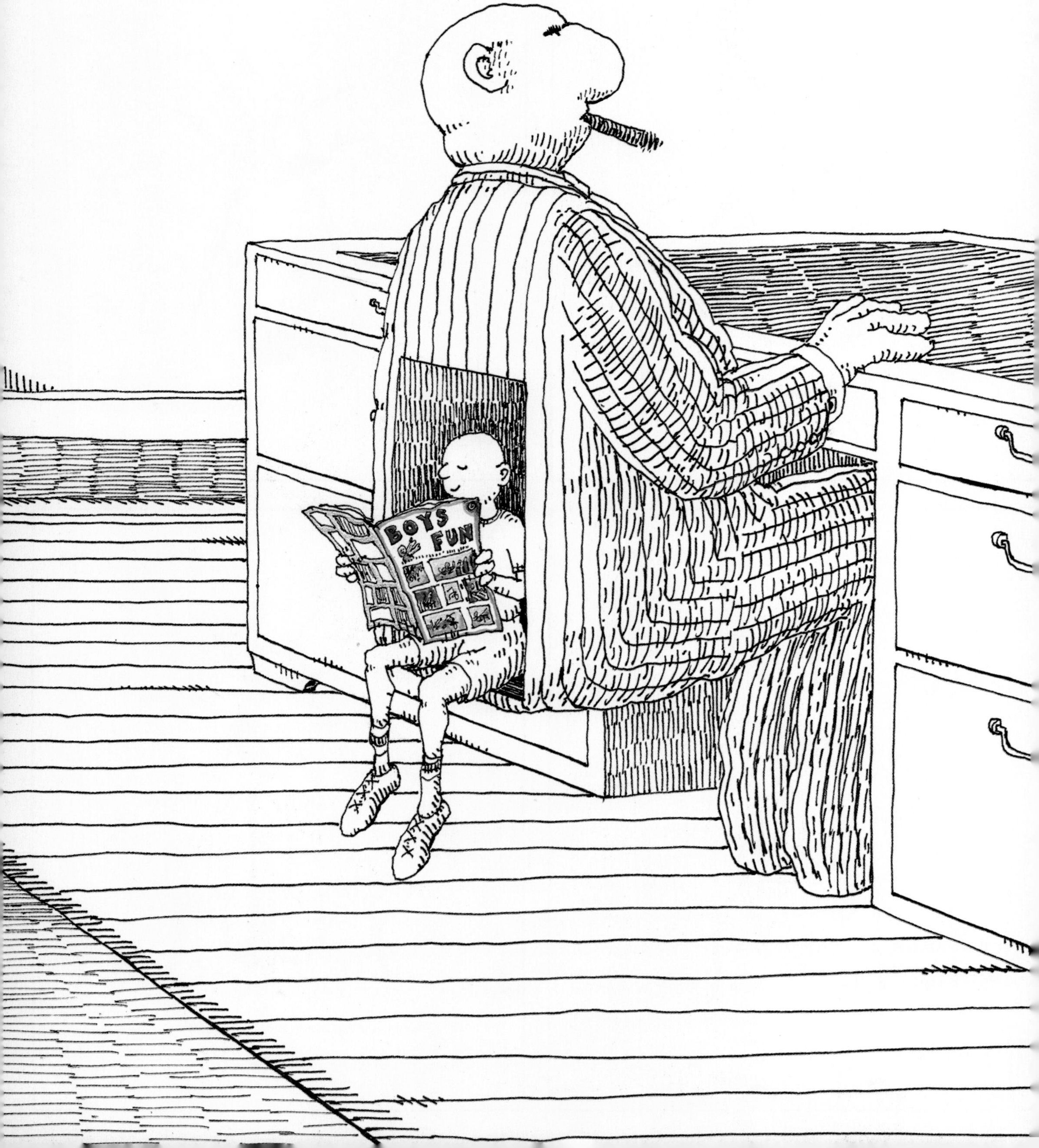
BOYS
FUN

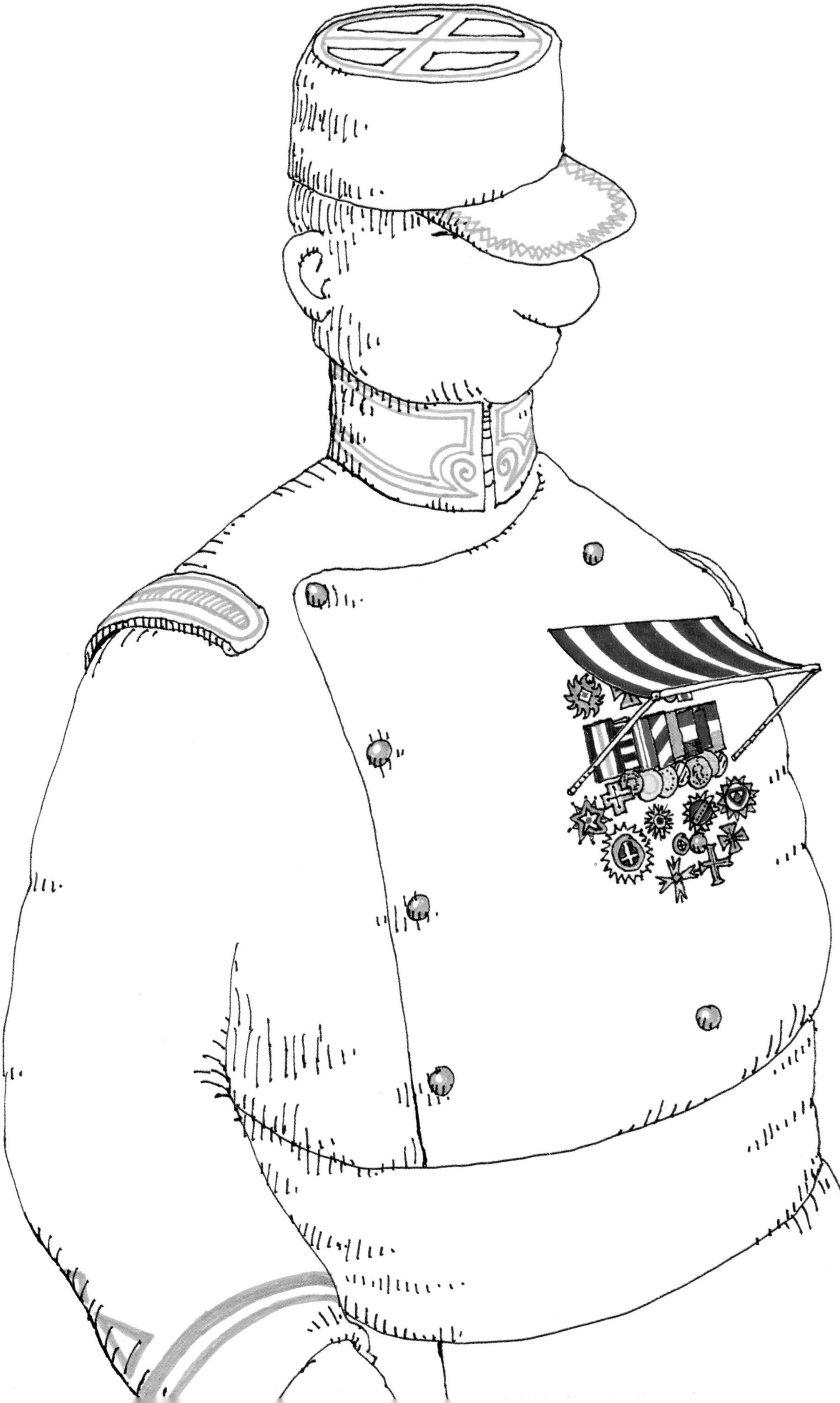